ESTHER

A Woman of Strength & Dignity

BIBLE STUDY GUIDE

From the Bible-teaching ministry of

CHARLES R. SWINDOLL

INSIGHT FOR LIVING

Chuck graduated in 1963 from Dallas Theological Seminary, where he now serves as the school's fourth president, helping to prepare a new generation of men and women for the ministry. Chuck has served in pastorates in three states: Massachusetts, Texas, and California, including almost twenty-three years at the First Evangelical Free Church in Fullerton, California. His sermon messages have been aired over radio since 1979 as the *Insight for Living* broadcast. A best-selling author, Chuck has written numerous books and booklets on many subjects.

Based on the outlines and transcripts of Chuck's sermons, the study guide text and the Living Insights sections are coauthored by Ken Gire, a graduate of Texas Christian University and Dallas Theological Seminary. The Questions for Group Discussion are coauthored by Bryce Klabunde, a graduate of Biola University and Dallas Theological Seminary.

Editor in Chief:	**Text Designer:**
Cynthia Swindoll	Gary Lett
Senior Editor:	**Graphics System Administrator:**
Bryce Klabunde	Bob Haskins
Assistant Editor:	**Director, Communications Division:**
Wendy Peterson	John Norton
Copy Editors:	**Production Coordinator:**
Deborah Gibbs	Don Bernstein
Marco Salazar	**Project Coordinator:**
	Colette Muse

Unless otherwise identified, all Scripture references are from the New American Standard Bible, updated edition, copyright © The Lockman Foundation 1960, 1962, 1963, 1968, 1971, 1972, 1973, 1975, 1977, 1995. Used by permission.

Scripture taken from the Holy Bible, New International Version © 1973, 1978, 1984 International Bible Society, used by permission of Zondervan Bible Publishers [NIV]. The other translations cited are the *King James Version* [KJV], *The Living Bible* [LB], and *The New Testament in Modern English* [PHILLIPS].

Guide titled *Esther: A Woman for Such a Time as This* coauthored by Ken Gire:
Copyright © 1990 by Charles R. Swindoll, Inc.

Guide title was changed to *Esther: A Woman of Strength and Dignity* when Charles R. Swindoll wrote the book by that title in 1997.

Revised edition: Questions for Group Discussion authored by Bryce Klabunde:
Copyright © 1997 by Charles R. Swindoll, Inc.

Original outlines, charts, and transcripts:
Copyright © 1989 by Charles R. Swindoll, Inc.

An effort has been made to locate sources and obtain permission where necessary for the quotations used in this book. In the event of any unintentional omission, a modification will gladly be incorporated in future printings.

ISBN 1-57972-058-7
STUDY GUIDE COVER DESIGN: Gary Lett. Adapted from the hardback cover design by D^2 Design Works; hardback illustration by Linda Fennimore.
Printed in the United States of America

CONTENTS

INTRODUCTION

I have a confession to make. Not until I undertook this verse-by-verse exposition of Esther had I ever made a serious study of her life. I knew who she was, and I understood, in a general manner, the plot of her story; but little did I realize how beautifully it fit into our own times.

Now that the work is complete, I cannot describe the depth of my gratitude for this rather obscure and often-overlooked book in the Old Testament. As you work your way through these chapters, you will be amazed at the relevance of each message. Though God's name does not once appear in the book, His hand is on every life and His will is in every decision. You will love the way He sovereignly weaves the threads of His purpose through the events that transpire.

So . . . welcome to another opportunity to discover truth to live by from an ancient scroll most people have never even read. It won't be long before you will be enchanted by Esther's captivating charm and challenged by her unswerving courage.

Chuck Swindoll

Chuck Swindoll

PUTTING TRUTH
INTO ACTION

K nowledge apart from application falls short of God's desire for His children. He wants us to apply what we learn so that we will change and grow. This study guide was prepared with these goals in mind. As you go through the following pages, we hope your desire to discover biblical truth will grow as your understanding of God's Word increases and that you will be encouraged to apply what you've learned.

To assist you in your study, we've included a section called **Living Insights** at the end of each lesson. These exercises will challenge you to study further and to think of specific ways to put your discoveries into action.

In this edition, we've added **Questions for Group Discussion,** which are formulated to get your group talking about the key issues in each lesson.

There are many ways to use this guide—in personal devotions, group studies, discussions with friends and family, and Sunday school classes. And, of course, it's an ideal study aid when you're listening to its corresponding *Insight for Living* radio series.

To benefit most from this study guide, we would encourage you to consider it a spiritual journal. That's why we've included space in the **Living Insights** for recording your thoughts and discoveries. We hope you'll return to those sections often for review and encouragement as you continue to grow in your walk with Christ.

Ken Gire
Coauthor of Text
Author of Living Insights

Bryce Klabunde
Author of Group Discussion
Questions

ESTHER

A Woman of Strength & Dignity

ESTHER

God's providence among his people during . . .

. . . Hard Times

. . . Happy Times

	King's Banquet	Haman's Edict	Queen's Courage	God's Deliverance	Mordecai's Edict	Jews' Rejoicing	Shalom!
	Honoring the kingdom		Urging of Mordecai	Mordecai honored		Enemies destroyed	
	Honoring the new queen		Approaching the King	Haman hanged		Feast established	
	CHAPTERS 1–2	CHAPTER 3	CHAPTERS 4–5	CHAPTERS 6–7	CHAPTER 8	CHAPTER 9	CHAPTER 10

Circumstance	Threat and trust		Deliverance and praise
Feasts	of the king	of the queen	of the nation
Dates	483 B.C.		473 B.C.
Theme	The sovereign accomplishment of God's purposes through ordinary people and apparent coincidences		
Key Verses	4:12–16; 10:3		

Chapter 1

GOD'S INVINSIBLE PROVIDENCE

Survey of Esther

Although Shakespeare never appears in his plays, his presence is pervasive. Every act, every scene, every line of dialogue bears the imprint of his pen. He is the genius behind all the characters, each twist of plot, every poignant ending.

As far as the dramas in Scripture are concerned, the Book of Esther is an anomaly. It is the only book in the Bible that doesn't mention God's name. But like Shakespeare's plays, every page bears testimony to its author. Behind each scene you can see the shadow of the Almighty directing from the wings.

More than any other biblical book, Esther is a tribute to the invisible providence of God. Although we never actually hear or see God in the story, we have an overwhelming sense of confidence that He is just offstage, cueing the characters and orchestrating the drama in order to preserve His people from a tragic ending.

The Book of Esther is often like the dramas played out in our everyday lives. For seldom when enemies are on our heels are our Red Seas parted. Seldom when disaster is at our door are we warned by angelic visitors. Seldom when we are in need of direction are we instructed by God from a burning bush. And neither was Esther.

It's easy to see God in the miraculous. It's not so easy to see Him in the mundane. But that's where most of us live—without seeing handwriting on the wall or hearing thunder from Sinai. We live with God, not center stage, but directing unobtrusively from the wings.

This is all the more why we need to be sensitive to His voice—so we can be aware of and attentive to the subtle ways in which He works. And no book will sharpen our spiritual senses more than Esther.

Gaining a Deeper Understanding of God

A study of the Book of Esther is really a study of God's power and sovereignty. So as we begin, let's take a few soundings on the unfathomable subject of God. It's easy to put God in a box or relegate Him to an outline or a table of contents. But God refuses tidy summary. He refuses to be confined by our conventional wisdom. It's important to understand how mysterious God is if we are ever to make sense of the mysterious ways in which He works.

The Mind of God—His Unsearchable Judgments

Our searching the mind of God is a little like a minnow surveying the ocean. At best, we'll only see what lies in front of our tiny eyes, but we'll miss the depth and the breadth of its watery secrets. As Isaiah the prophet wrote:

> "For My thoughts are not your thoughts,
> Nor are your ways My ways," declares the Lord.
> "For as the heavens are higher than the earth,
> So are My ways higher than your ways
> And My thoughts than your thoughts."
> (Isa. 55:8–9)

The Will of God—His Unfathomable Ways

Like the unseen depths of the ocean, the ways of God are often cloaked in mystery.

> Oh, the depth of the riches both of the wisdom
> and knowledge of God! How unsearchable are His
> judgments and unfathomable His ways! For who has
> known the mind of the Lord, or who became His
> counselor? (Rom. 11:33–34)

The Power of God—His Sovereign Control

The power of God is beautifully described in a doxology in Daniel 4:34b–35.

> "For His dominion is an everlasting dominion,
> And His kingdom endures from generation to
> generation.
> All the inhabitants of the earth are accounted as
> nothing,

But He does according to His will in the host of
heaven
And among the inhabitants of earth;
And no one can ward off His hand
Or say to Him, 'What have You done?'"

These gilded words came on the heels of a humiliating journey that took King Nebuchadnezzar from insanity to recovery. Once pretentiously robed in his own pride, the king was stripped of his sanity and made to see who really ruled heaven and earth. Having been crushed under the mighty hand of God, the king finally acknowledged the pervasiveness of God's power.

The Presence of God—His Invisible Providence

The word *provident* is derived from the Latin word *providēre*. The prefix *pro* means "before"; the root *vidēre* means "I see." As monarch over heaven and earth, God sees events before they happen. He can see the future with precise clarity because He is the One who works events according to His perfect plan.

Therefore, even when things appear to be out of hand or off course, God is there, working invisibly behind the scenes (see Eccles. 7:13–14). Even though the seasons change dramatically, even though nations rise and fall on the world landscape, and even though economies tower to prosperity or topple to ruin, God never changes. From everlasting to everlasting, He is God, and His kingdom remains unshakable (Ps. 46; 90:1–2; Isa. 40:6–8).

Make no mistake about it. God will have His way. Though He remains invisible, He is in no way indifferent.

Seeing the Invisible Workings of God

Before the curtain rises on the drama of Esther, and before the houselights dim, let's take a look at the playbill introducing us to the cast.

The Cast of Characters

The first is a king named Ahasuerus.

Now it took place in the days of Ahasuerus, the Ahasuerus who reigned from India to Ethiopia over 127 provinces, in those days as King Ahasuerus sat on his royal throne which was at the citadel in Susa. (Esther 1:1–2)

This king is also known in Scripture as Xerxes. He was a Persian king whose fame extended from India to Ethiopia; under his reign were thousands of Jews who had chosen not to return to Palestine under the direction of Zerubbabel. The word *Jews* is mentioned over fifty times in Esther, turning the spotlight on these members of the cast.

The second character in the cast is a queen named Vashti. She is a strong-willed, independent-minded woman who refuses to co-operate with her husband's drunken demands. We first meet her in 1:9.

> Queen Vashti also gave a banquet for the women in the palace which belonged to King Ahasuerus.

The third character to make his stage entrance is a man named Haman. He is the villain, a wicked, anti-Semitic officer in the king's court with a personal profile of conceit, wealth, influence, and deception. We see him profiled in chapter 3.

> After these events King Ahasuerus promoted Haman, the son of Hammedatha the Agagite, and advanced him and established his authority over all the princes who were with him. All the king's servants who were at the king's gate bowed down and paid homage to Haman; for so the king had commanded concerning him. But Mordecai neither bowed down nor paid homage. . . . Then the king took his signet ring from his hand and gave it to Haman, the son of Hammedatha the Agagite, the enemy of the Jews. (vv. 1–2, 10)

Playing opposite wicked Haman is a godly Jew named Mordecai. We are first introduced to him in 2:5–6.

> Now there was at the citadel in Susa a Jew whose name was Mordecai, the son of Jair, the son of Shimei, the son of Kish, a Benjamite, who had been taken into exile from Jerusalem with the captives who had been exiled with Jeconiah king of Judah, whom Nebuchadnezzar the king of Babylon had exiled.

We read in the very next verse that Mordecai raised the orphan Esther, who later turns out to be the heroine of the story.

> He was bringing up Hadassah, that is Esther, his

uncle's daughter, for she had no father or mother. Now the young lady was beautiful of form and face, and when her father and her mother died, Mordecai took her as his own daughter. (v. 7)

She was a lowly Jewish woman who was as dazzling in outer beauty as she was in inner beauty. In fact, her name is the Persian name for "star," and she later ascended to the throne as queen after Vashti had a meteoric fall from the king's grace.

The Plot of the Book

The plot of Esther revolves around the survival of the Jews, who stood precariously on the threshold of a holocaust.

Mordecai's refusal to pay Haman homage enrages the petty leader so much that he determines to make the whole Jewish population pay with their lives (3:2b–6, 8–13). Word of their impending doom spreads throughout the Jewish community (4:1–3). Realizing that the fate of his people hangs by the thread of Esther's relationship to the king, Mordecai appeals to the queen.

He asks her to do a courageous thing—to stand alone before the king (vv. 13–17). Rising to the occasion of her need, God grants Esther the wisdom to devise a strategy that will eliminate the archenemy of her people. She invites both Haman and the king to a banquet where the king has vowed to hear what is troubling the queen and grant her wish (5:6–8).

Meanwhile, Haman is elated at the invitation. But as he passes the defiant Mordecai, who again refuses to pay him homage, his elation turns to infuriation. And at the advice of his wife, Haman erects a gallows from which he plans to hang Mordecai (vv. 12–14).

God, however, providentially uses insomnia to awaken in the king an awareness of Mordecai's past heroism—heroism that had once saved the king's life. He decides that Mordecai should be exalted (6:1–10). So instead of putting a noose around Mordecai's neck, Haman is ordered to drape a robe of honor over his shoulders. Haman comes to the royal banquet, stewing over the sudden reversal of Mordecai's fate. Little does he realize the hot water he is about to be in. At the table, Esther reveals the plot against her people. The king asks the perpetrator's identity, and Esther points her finger at Haman. In a sudden rage, the king sentences the archvillain to be hanged. And hanged he is—on the very gallows he had erected for Mordecai (7:10).

Though God is invisible, He is invincible. As the hymnwriter proclaimed, "Immortal, invisible, God only wise."[1] That is the message of the Book of Esther. The invisible God who may appear to be absent is the invincible God who is working out His wise plan.

That is not only true for a young woman and her people in ancient Persia; that's true for us today. Go back to Esther 7:10 and let your mind linger over the incredible reversal of fates—those of Haman and Mordecai.

The gallows stood like a seven-and-a-half-story skeleton, gaunt and waiting. Haman was strategically positioned in the government to grease the gears of the political machine to obliterate the Jewish people. Unknown to the king's court, Mordecai was first on the list of political dissidents to be disposed of. Yet through Esther, a beautiful but inexperienced ingenue, God's invincible providence turned everything around.

Responding to the Quiet Promptings of God

Esther realized that God had raised her to a position of prominence for a reason. But to understand that reason, she had to ignore her palatial surroundings and listen to the still, small voice of Providence. Psalm 46 commands us to do the same. It is a terse command of only eight words, yet those eight simple words are revolutionary: "Be still, and know that I am God" (v. 10a KJV). The New American Standard Bible translates it, "'Cease striving and know that I am God.'" The Living Bible says, "'Stand silent! . . .'" The Hebrew literally means, "Let go, relax."

What will happen when we do? We'll learn what Esther learned —that God, though invisible, is invincible. But we will only learn that if we listen.

> Whoever will listen will hear the speaking Heaven.
> This is definitely not the hour when men take kindly
> to an exhortation to listen, for listening is not today
> a part of popular religion. We are at the opposite
> end of the pole from there. Religion has accepted
> the monstrous heresy that noise, size, activity and

---

1. Walter Chalmers Smith, "Immortal, Invisible, God Only Wise," in *Hymns for the Family of God* (Nashville, Tenn.: Paragon Associates, 1976), no. 319.

bluster make a man dear to God. But we may take heart. To a people caught in the tempest of the last great conflict God says, "Be still, and know that I am God" (Ps. 46:10), and still He says it, as if He means to tell us that our strength and safety lie not in noise but in silence.[2]

Certainly that was true for the strength and safety of the Jewish nation under Ahasuerus. And certainly that is true for us as well.

Living Insights

In Psalm 46, the world is being dashed apart by earthquakes and tidal waves. Yet in the midst of that calamitous uncertainty, the psalmist discovers one thing he can count on—God. He can cease his striving because "The Lord of hosts is with us; The God of Jacob is our stronghold" (v. 11).

Perhaps the world you live in is falling apart around you as well. You may be facing a life-threatening illness or major surgery. Your body may be twisted from debilitating pain. You may carry unbearable emotional stress home with you from work. If you're a student, you may be buried under the books. Maybe you suffer the sharp pain of a fractured relationship—one you've tried to restore, but it just won't mend. Maybe your career is uncertain or your job security precarious. Maybe you're in a moral war with yourself and you're already feeling the incriminating introspection of defeat.

Whatever mountains are crumbling around you, take the high ground and stop striving. *Initially, be quiet.* Listen to the whisper of God behind the roar of your circumstances. You can hear Him, even in the whirlwind, but you have to be still to listen. Then, *ultimately, be convinced.* God may change your circumstances as He did for Esther and Mordecai. Most of all, though, He wants to change you. Be assured that God is for you, not against you; that He is working behind the scenes for your highest good (Rom. 8:28–30).

In the following space, write down what you hear when you calm yourself to listen to the still, quiet voice of God beneath the roar of your circumstances.

2. A. W. Tozer, *The Pursuit of God*, The Tozer Legacy Edition (Camp Hill, Pa.: Christian Publications, 1982), p. 80.

_____

_____

_____

_____

_____

_____

_____

_____

_____

_____

Questions for Group Discussion

1. Esther's story demonstrates that God doesn't need to reveal Himself for us to know He's there. Like the wind, He moves invisibly through our lives, sometimes softly reassuring us of His presence, sometimes powerfully altering the landscape of our circumstances. Do you ever question whether God is really involved in your life? If so, when do your doubts most often emerge?

2. Why do you think God often chooses to work in an "invisible" way?

3. Although God remains hidden in the Book of Esther, the plot twists and "coincidences" clearly reveal His hand at work. Where do you see God's hand in the twists and turns of your life's story?

4. When Ahasuerus signed the edict, he sealed the fate of thousands of Jews . . . or so it seemed. Through an amazing reversal of destinies, God turned the death edict into a life-saving victory for the Jews. A similar reversal occurred at the Cross. How did God turn what Satan had meant for evil into something good?

5. What have you learned about God in this chapter that can help you trust Him more during life's threatening circumstances?

Chapter 2

THERE SHE GOES...
MISS PERSIA!
Esther 1:1–2:7

Winston Churchill had an appointment with Destiny. But he was oblivious to the calendar Destiny kept—that is, until May 10, 1939, when he discovered his name inked in its appointment book.

The morning of May 10 dawned in London with news of a German offensive. Holland and Belgium had been invaded, and France would soon be trodden under by the rapidly advancing Nazi boot.

At six o'clock that morning a message summoned Churchill to the royal palace. There the king asked him to mobilize the government against Hitler. By the end of the day Churchill had accepted a position he would hold for the duration of the war, one that would secure him a place of honor in history.

His journal records his feelings of that fateful night.

> During these last crowded days of the political crisis, my pulse had not quickened at any moment. I took it all as it came. But I cannot conceal from the reader of this truthful account that as I went to bed at about 3 A.M. I was conscious of a profound sense of relief. At last I had the authority to give directions over the whole scene. I felt as if I were walking with Destiny, and that all my past life had been but a preparation for this hour and for this trial.[1]

Certainly Esther must have felt similarly when she heard the fateful words of Mordecai:

> "For if you remain silent at this time, relief and deliverance will arise for the Jews from another place and you and your father's house will perish. And who knows whether you have not attained royalty for such a time as this?" (Esther 4:14)

---

1. Winston Churchill, quoted in *Turning Point*, ed. Philip Dunaway and George de Kay (New York, N.Y.: Random House, 1958), p. 284.

"For such a time as this"—Esther's appointment with Destiny. Like Churchill, her whole life had been "but a preparation for this hour and for this trial." And now was the time for her to step forward and keep that appointment.

Uneventful Beginnings—Unbelievable Endings

Esther went from the humdrum life of an orphan to the palatial life of a queen. From there she went on to become a heroine and secure a place of honor in Israel's history. Unbelievable, isn't it?

The New Testament records a number of incidents that started uneventfully yet ended unbelievably. The birth of our Lord is one. The night was like any night. There were no handbills passed announcing the birth. There was no reception by the city fathers. Yet on that silent night in Bethlehem, God entered the world. And since then, the ripples of that event have touched every shore on the face of the earth.

Another incident was the day of Christ's resurrection. Just another sleepy Sunday morning for the majority of people in Jerusalem. And yet that chilly pastel morning gave a dawn of hope to a world shrouded in the dark finality of the grave.

The day of Christ's return will be another day that starts out routinely. Alarm clocks will go off as usual. People will bustle off on their normal schedules—to work, to school, to appointments. But suddenly, curtains of clouds will part and the Lord Himself will descend dramatically.

The Old Testament has some equally compelling examples. The day the great Flood swallowed every civilization on earth. The day Moses encountered the burning bush and was commissioned to lead the Exodus. The day a simple young shepherd boy named David was anointed by Samuel to be king.

Esther's Uneventful Beginning

God is still in the business of bringing about unbelievable endings from uneventful beginnings. What seems mundane to you now may simply be the preparation for something monumental—the way it was for Esther.

Little did this insignificant orphan girl know the incredible way God would work in her life. When she crawled out of bed that day with mussed hair and morning breath, little did she realize that she would be selected to enter a beauty pageant whose prize would be the queen's throne of the Medo-Persian Empire.

The Book of Esther begins blandly enough: "Now it took place in the days of Ahasuerus . . ." The Hebrew is just as lackluster: "And it was . . ." The NIV captures the ordinariness of the beginning with the words, "This is what happened . . ." But what follows is anything but dull.

A Casual Glimpse into a Persian Palace

Verses 1–2 set the stage for the resplendent opening scene.

> Now it took place in the days of Ahasuerus, the Ahasuerus who reigned from India to Ethiopia over 127 provinces, in those days as King Ahasuerus sat on his royal throne which was at the citadel in Susa.

What took place? A party . . . and what a party!

> In the third year of his reign he gave a banquet for all his princes and attendants, the army officers of Persia and Media, the nobles and the princes of his provinces being in his presence. And he displayed the riches of his royal glory and the splendor of his great majesty for many days, 180 days.
>
> When these days were completed, the king gave a banquet lasting seven days for all the people who were present at the citadel in Susa, from the greatest to the least, in the court of the garden of the king's palace. There were hangings of fine white and violet linen held by cords of fine purple linen on silver rings and marble columns, and couches of gold and silver on a mosaic pavement of porphyry, marble, mother-of-pearl and precious stones. Drinks were served in golden vessels of various kinds, and the royal wine was plentiful according to the king's bounty. The drinking was done according to the law, there was no compulsion, for so the king had given orders to each official of his household that he should do according to the desires of each person. (vv. 3–8)

Meanwhile, the king's wife threw a party of her own.

> Queen Vashti also gave a banquet for the women in the palace which belonged to King Ahasuerus. (v. 9)

11

A Public Conflict between the King and Queen

After a week of festivities, the stag party Ahasuerus hosted for the men got out of hand.

> On the seventh day, when the heart of the king was merry with wine, he commanded Mehuman, Biztha, Harbona, Bigtha, Abagtha, Zethar and Carkas, the seven eunuchs who served in the presence of King Ahasuerus, to bring Queen Vashti before the king with her royal crown in order to display her beauty to the people and the princes, for she was beautiful. (vv. 10–11)

The word translated *crown* literally means "turban." Some Jewish scholars suggest that the command was for Vashti to come unveiled to show off her beautiful face. Others suggest that the command was for her to come wearing only the turban, thus showing off everything.[2]

Vashti refused to come (v. 12a). Commentator Alexander Whyte describes her dignified response.

> Whatever the royal order that came to her out of the banqueting-hall exactly was, the brave queen refused to obey it. Her beauty was her own and her husband's: it was not for open show among hundreds of half-drunk men.[3]

Queen Vashti represents a good example of the limits of a wife's submission. The command for a wife to submit to her husband is clear in Scripture (see Eph. 5:22–24). But it is not absolute and without limits. The woman does not give up her dignity as a human being when she becomes a wife. Neither should she allow her principles to be trodden underfoot by an unprincipled husband. Marriage does not give the husband license to pursue his basest sexual fantasies, and neither does it enslave the wife to fulfill them.

Nevertheless, the queen's refusal infuriated the king and spurred a heated debate about the effect her actions might have on Persian society's status quo.

---

2. F. B. Huey Jr., "Esther," in *The Expositor's Bible Commentary*, gen. ed. Frank E. Gaebelein (Grand Rapids, Mich.: Zondervan Publishing House, 1988), vol. 4, p. 800.

3. Alexander Whyte, *Bible Characters* (London, England: Oliphants, 1952), vol. 1, p. 419.

Then the king became very angry and his wrath burned within him.

Then the king said to the wise men who understood the times—for it was the custom of the king so to speak before all who knew law and justice and were close to him: Carshena, Shethar, Admatha, Tarshish, Meres, Marsena and Memucan, the seven princes of Persia and Media who had access to the king's presence and sat in the first place in the kingdom—"According to law, what is to be done with Queen Vashti, because she did not obey the command of King Ahasuerus delivered by the eunuchs?" In the presence of the king and the princes, Memucan said, "Queen Vashti has wronged not only the king but also all the princes and all the peoples who are in all the provinces of King Ahasuerus. For the queen's conduct will become known to all the women causing them to look with contempt on their husbands by saying, 'King Ahasuerus commanded Queen Vashti to be brought in to his presence, but she did not come.' This day the ladies of Persia and Media who have heard of the queen's conduct will speak in the same way to all the king's princes, and there will be plenty of contempt and anger." (Esther 1:12b–18)

Immediate Proclamation for All to Obey

Emerging from the fear that men might lose control of their wives, Memucan's advice revealed two agendas: demean the queen (v. 19), and continue the domination of women throughout the Persian Empire (vv. 20–22).

"If it pleases the king, let a royal edict be issued by him and let it be written in the laws of Persia and Media so that it cannot be repealed, that Vashti may no longer come into the presence of King Ahasuerus, and let the king give her royal position to another who is more worthy than she.[4] When the

4. Because Vashti refused to come into his presence, the king banished her from his presence forever.

king's edict which he shall make is heard throughout all his kingdom, great as it is, then all women will give honor to their husbands, great and small."

This word pleased the king and the princes, and the king did as Memucan proposed. So he sent letters to all the king's provinces, to each province according to its script and to every people according to their language, that every man should be the master in his own house and the one who speaks in the language of his own people.[5] (vv. 19–22)

As far as God's providence was concerned, the most important point of the edict was, "Let the king give her royal position to another." That clause prepared the way for Esther. And it illustrates the truth of Proverbs 21:1.

> The king's heart is like channels of water in the
>   hand of the Lord;
> He turns it wherever He wishes.

The gears of providence may grind slowly, but they track perfectly the sovereign course the Lord has designed for them. And nobody—not even a powerful king—can stand in their way.

A Lingering Loneliness and a Creative Idea

Esther 2 begins in a wistful, almost melancholy, tone.

> After these things when the anger of King Ahasuerus had subsided, he remembered Vashti and what she had done and what had been decreed against her. (v. 1)

"After these things" is vague—after what things? It was probably shortly after Ahasuerus had suffered defeat in the wars he waged against Greece in 480–479 B.C.[6] This lapse of time would have given the king's anger toward Vashti a chance to subside, leaving him lonely and nostalgic. It had been awhile since Ahasuerus had

---

5. With his edict, the king thought he had the last word. Ironically, God would use a woman, Esther, to "master" him by turning his heart against Haman.

6. "Between the events of 1:3 and 2:16, Xerxes [Ahasuerus] made his disastrous expedition to Greece. Returning from his naval defeat at Salamis in 480 and his humiliating rout at Plataea in 479, he turned his thoughts to remarriage, through which he hoped to find solace." Huey, "Esther," p. 804.

enjoyed the companionship of a queen, and he was despondent. His attendants took note of the lingering loneliness and prescribed a remedy.

> Then the king's attendants, who served him, said, "Let beautiful young virgins be sought for the king. Let the king appoint overseers in all the provinces of his kingdom that they may gather every beautiful young virgin to the citadel of Susa, to the harem, into the custody of Hegai, the king's eunuch, who is in charge of the women; and let their cosmetics be given them.[7] Then let the young lady who pleases the king be queen in place of Vashti." And the matter pleased the king, and he did accordingly. (vv. 2–4)

An Unknown Man—An Obscure Woman

A Medo-Persian beauty pageant almost seems something to raise eyebrows over, but God used it providentially to merge Esther's path with Ahasuerus'.

> Now there was at the citadel in Susa a Jew whose name was Mordecai, the son of Jair, the son of Shimei, the son of Kish, a Benjamite, who had been taken into exile from Jerusalem with the captives who had been exiled with Jeconiah king of Judah, whom Nebuchadnezzar the king of Babylon had exiled. He was bringing up Hadassah, that is Esther, his uncle's daughter, for she had no father or mother. Now the young lady was beautiful of form and face, and when her father and her mother died, Mordecai took her as his own daughter. (vv. 5–7)

See how this contestant's resume reads? She was a Jew and an orphan, raised by her cousin. Not much else is recorded about her— except that she was shapely and stunning. Yet, as we will see, she became the queen who would save the Jews from complete annihilation.

---

7. The Hebrew root "to rub, to polish, signifies purification and adornment with all kind of precious ointments." C. F. Keil, "I and II Kings, I and II Chronicles, Ezra, Nehemiah, Esther," *Commentary on the Old Testament in Ten Volumes,* by C. F. Keil and F. Delitzsch (Grand Rapids, Mich.: William B. Eerdmans Publishing Co., n.d.), vol. 3, p. 334. See also Esther 2:12.

How God Still Works in Uneventful Times

Esther's life is a classic example of an uneventful beginning that led to an unbelievable ending. But that was ancient history. What about today? Does God still work through uneventful beginnings?

You bet He does. And here are three thoughts to keep in mind when you're muddling through a mundane Monday morning.

God's plans are not hindered when events are secular or carnal. His power penetrates through the broken glass of a drunken banquet as well as through the stained glass of a Gothic cathedral.

God's purposes are not frustrated by moral or marital conflicts. The king, in all his drunken debauchery and cruel chauvinism, could not thwart the purposes of God. In reality, he was not king at all, but only one more pawn in the hand of God. And God could move him anywhere on the chessboard that He wanted (see Prov. 21:1).

God's people are not excluded from high places because of handicap or hardship. Esther was a foreigner and an orphan. By all human odds it was a million-to-one chance that she would even be invited to the pageant, let alone win it. But by God's providence, it happened.

Hebrews 11:1 says, "Faith is the assurance of things hoped for, the conviction of things not seen." Throughout the marbled halls of that chapter in Hebrews are statues of ordinary men and women who believed God in extraordinary ways. Many lived much of their lives as Esther did, in uneventful times. Yet from Abraham dwelling in tents to David tending sheep, God providentially worked to script unbelievable endings to the stories of their lives.

Want to hear something even more incredible? God wants to do the same with your life.

Living Insights

A character in this story who is often overshadowed by Esther is Queen Vashti. Whatever else may be said about her, she was a woman of conviction. She stood up to the most powerful man in the land at the expense of her marriage and her throne.

Not many people would be able to stand so firm in their convictions. How about you? Does any principle mean so much to you that you would be willing to risk losing your job over it? Is there any principle for which you would be willing to risk a significant relationship?

Most of us tend to live by expedience rather than by principle, making decisions not on the basis of our convictions but on the basis of possible consequences. Dietrich Bonhoeffer, however, opposed this thinking: "If we claim to be Christians, there is no room for expediency."[8]

Describe a time when you compromised your convictions because of the consequences you thought would result.

_____

_____

_____

_____

Looking back, how do you feel about that incident?

_____

_____

_____

_____

Joseph is an inspiring Old Testament example of someone who lived by his convictions rather than by anticipated consequences (see Gen. 39). Turning to the New Testament, we find another stirring example in Stephen (Acts 6:8–7:60). If you fear the consequences of standing up for your convictions, read Romans 8:31–39 for encouragement.

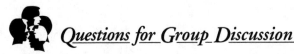 ## Questions for Group Discussion

1. The Book of Esther opens with a magnificent celebration. On parade was the best humankind had to offer, from the marble-columned architecture to the sumptuous spreads of food. What do you think was the purpose of King Ahasuerus' grand banquet?

2. As the revelry stretched into weeks and then months, the elegant

---

8. As quoted by G. Leibholz in "Memoir," in Dietrich Bonhoeffer's *The Cost of Discipleship*, rev. ed. (1949; reprint, New York, N.Y.: Macmillan Co., 1963), p. 25.

gala disintegrated into a drunken bash. In the final climactic week, the palace doors swung open to everyone in Susa in an unrestrained Mardi Gras (see Esther 1:5–8). What started as an exhibition of the best of humankind turned into a display of the worst. What does that tell you about human nature?

3. Intoxicated by the wine and his overindulged pride, Ahasuerus summoned Vashti "in order to display her beauty to the people and the princes" (v. 11). What do you think was behind his command? Why would the king want to show off his queen to the people?

4. Was Vashti right to refuse her husband's wishes?

5. When is it right for a wife to say no to her husband?

6. Vashti's refusal dealt the king's ego a serious blow. The "master" of the kingdom could not master his own wife. Memucan said that Queen Vashti "wronged" the king by not coming when he asked (v. 16). But wasn't *she* the one wronged? What kept the king from admitting his mistake?

7. How do you treat those you love? Do you ever try to control or take advantage of them for your own purposes? What sometimes keeps you from admitting you're wrong?

8. Out of the ugliness of Esther 1—the debauchery, pride, lust, indignity, anger—blooms the beauty of Esther 2. Share how God has turned a bad situation in your life into something good and hopeful.

Chapter 3

STRENGTH AND DIGNITY ON PARADE

Esther 2:8–20

There is truth in the age-old maxim "The hand that rocks the cradle rules the world." That hand is the strong yet tender one of a mother, who not only bears the children but rears them as well. It is no wonder that when the cameras are turned on the 250-pound football player who's just scored a touchdown or recovered a fumble, the first words to come out of his mouth are "Hi, Mom!"

But as if raising a houseful of children isn't enough of a job, the married woman has at least one other demanding career—that of a wife. She is there for her husband either as the wind beneath his wings or the one who lets the air out of his tires. Proverbs talks about both kinds of wives. The ideal is the excellent wife of Proverbs 31. Her worth is far above jewels; her husband can entrust his heart to her completely because "she does him good and not evil All the days of her life" (vv. 11–12).

Such a woman, one who fears the Lord, will be praised (v. 30). And such a woman was Esther.

God-Given Strengths Found in Women

Over the course of her life, Esther demonstrated four strengths more often seen in women than men:

intuition—the ability to see through situations, sense the unspoken, perceive the feelings underneath the surface

endurance—the ability to handle pain, stay at a task through insuperable odds, persevere

responsiveness—the willingness to express feelings, respond to others, show warmth and affection

vulnerability—the courage to confess weakness, admit fear, ask for help

Esther also exemplified Proverbs' truths about a godly woman's value and strengths.

A gracious woman attains honor. (11:16a)

An excellent wife is the crown of her husband. (12:4a)

He who finds a wife finds a good thing
And obtains favor from the Lord. (18:22)

House and wealth are an inheritance from fathers,
But a prudent wife is from the Lord. (19:14)

As we enter this next, crucial portion of Esther's life, we'll see her chosen as the king's wife—and she'll be "the crown of her husband" indeed.

Esther: The King's Favorite . . . and Why

Let's pick up Esther's story in the powder room of the palace, where the contestants are putting on their makeup for the Miss Persia pageant.

> So it came about when the command and decree of the king were heard and many young ladies were gathered to the citadel of Susa into the custody of Hegai, that Esther was taken to the king's palace into the custody of Hegai, who was in charge of the women. (Esther 2:8)

The verb *was taken* doesn't connote volunteerism. In fact, this verb can mean "taken by force." Some Jewish scholars accept this interpretation, although there is nothing in the text to reinforce that idea. However, it could well be that Esther was reluctant to participate.[1] After all, she was a Jew, and becoming a concubine or marrying a Gentile was against the code of conduct handed down from early Jewish law (see Deut. 7:1–6).

When you imagine how competitive the contestants must have been at the prospect of being chosen queen, Esther's reluctance must have come across as wonderfully unique. Undoubtedly, Esther's inner beauty eclipsed the jealous, greedy, self-absorbed women of the harem, and that's what caught Hegai's eye. In the passages that follow, at least six of her attractive qualities stand out.

---

1. F. B. Huey Jr., "Esther," in *The Expositor's Bible Commentary* gen. ed. Frank E. Gaebelein (Grand Rapids, Mich.: Zondervan Publishing House, 1988), vol. 4, p. 806.

The first one is *a grace-filled charm and elegance*.

> Now the young lady pleased him and found favor with him. So he quickly provided her with her cosmetics and food, gave her seven choice maids from the king's palace and transferred her and her maids to the best place in the harem. (v. 9)

In Hebrew, the first sentence in verse 9 literally states: "She lifted up grace before his face."[2] Her manner exuded a pleasantness in the presence of others. So fragrant was this quality that its aroma prompted Hegai to act "quickly" and to treat her preferentially.

The second quality is *an unusual restraint and control*.

> Esther did not make known her people or her kindred. (v. 10a)

Esther knew the value of verbal restraint. Even when she became queen, she kept the secret Mordecai had told her to keep (see v. 20). That must have created not only an air of mystery about her but an aura of charm as well.

The third characteristic is *a continually teachable spirit*.

> For Mordecai had instructed her that she should not make them known. (v. 10b)

Becoming a finalist in this beauty pageant didn't go to Esther's head, and neither would becoming queen. Isn't it lovely to come across a woman of such stunning beauty who also has such a teachable spirit, such a willingness to listen and learn? Sometimes the more gifted we are—or the more physically endowed, the more popular, the more prominent in position—the less teachable we become. Which is unfortunate, because none of those gifts gives us a corner on wisdom.

The fourth quality is *an unselfish modesty and authenticity*.

> Now when the turn of each young lady came to go in to King Ahasuerus, after the end of her twelve months under the regulations for the women—for the days of their beautification were completed as follows: six months with oil of myrrh and six months with spices and the cosmetics for women—the young lady would go in to the king in this way: anything

2. Huey, "Esther," p. 806.

21

that she desired was given her to take with her from the harem to the king's palace. In the evening she would go in and in the morning she would return to the second harem, to the custody of Shaashgaz, the king's eunuch who was in charge of the concubines. She would not again go in to the king unless the king delighted in her and she was summoned by name.[3] (vv. 12–14)

Clearly, the process of preparing for a night with the king was lengthy and expensive. Imagine the setting: it must have been like going into Nordstrom or Neiman-Marcus and being able to take any of the dresses off the rack, any of the jewelry from the showcases, and a whole line of cosmetic products—all at no cost. No doubt, most of the women went on an extravagant and unrestrained shopping spree. Except for Esther.

Now when the turn of Esther, the daughter of Abihail the uncle of Mordecai who had taken her as his daughter, came to go in to the king, she did not request anything except what Hegai, the king's eunuch who was in charge of the women, advised. And Esther found favor in the eyes of all who saw her. (v. 15)

The fifth quality is *a winsomeness, regardless of her surroundings.* Did you note in verse 15 that Esther made no extravagant demands? She listened attentively to Hegai and followed his advice. Her winsomeness and charm not only compelled Hegai but totally captivated the king. Compared to the other women in the harem, she stood out in Ahasuerus' eyes like a stately swan in a duck pond.

So Esther was taken to King Ahasuerus to his royal palace in the tenth month which is the month Tebeth, in the seventh year of his reign.
The king loved Esther more than all the women, and she found favor and kindness with him more than all the virgins, so that he set the royal crown on her head and made her queen instead of Vashti. (vv. 16–17)

3. The women's futures rested on that one night with the king. As Huey notes, "Those rejected lived the rest of their lives like widows," "Esther," p. 808.

The sixth quality is *a humble respect for authority.*

> Then the king gave a great banquet, Esther's banquet, for all his princes and his servants; he also made a holiday for the provinces and gave gifts according to the king's bounty.
>
> When the virgins were gathered together the second time, then Mordecai was sitting at the king's gate. Esther had not yet made known her kindred or her people, even as Mordecai had commanded her; for Esther did what Mordecai told her as she had done when under his care. (vv. 18–20)

Now was Esther's golden opportunity to revel in her newly acquired position as queen, to throw off the shackles of accountability. But she resisted the temptation. She still submitted to Mordecai's counsel—a course of action that would later catapult her to the heights of heroism.

Practical Counsel for Modern-Day Esthers

The primary applications for this lesson appear to be aimed at women, but the principles run deeper than gender distinctions. They apply to men as well, for the cultivation of character is the focal point of our study. We're addressing what we are on the inside, not how we appear on the outside. So if you'll turn on the lights and squint in the mirror, we'll see what can be done for that hidden person of the heart.

First, *ask God to cultivate within you a discontent with the superficial and a desire for the spiritual.* Anne Morrow Lindbergh says it best in her excellent book *Gift from the Sea:*

> I am seeking perhaps what Socrates asked for in the prayer from the *Phaedrus* when he said, "May the outward and inward man be at one." I would like to achieve a state of inner spiritual grace from which I could function and give as I was meant to in the eye of God.[4]

Second, *trust God to control the circumstances around you.* Remember Esther. The atmosphere of such a competitive "beauty

4. Anne Morrow Lindbergh, *Gift from the Sea* (New York, N.Y.: Pantheon Books, 1955), pp. 23–24.

pageant" is a difficult one in which to preserve the beauty of the inner self. Yet in this soil, Esther blossomed.

Living Insights

In 1 Peter 3:3–4, the apostle exhorts women not to gild the outward picture frame but to concentrate on painting a masterpiece on the canvas of the inner person.

> Your adornment must not be merely external— braiding the hair, and wearing gold jewelry, or putting on dresses; but let it be the hidden person of the heart, with the imperishable quality of a gentle and quiet spirit, which is precious in the sight of God.

Peter isn't suggesting that it's wrong for a woman to fix her hair or wear jewelry. Rather, he's urging women to measure their beauty by more than what they see in the mirror.

What is the contrast between verses 3 and 4?

_____

_____

How would you define "a gentle and quiet spirit"?

_____

_____

Read Isaiah 3:16–26, and describe God's reaction to our focusing too much on external appearances.

_____

_____

What does our exclusive and intense focus on the physical reflect about ourselves (see v. 16a)?

_____

_____

From 1 Samuel 16:7, what is God's focus, and how can you begin to adorn that part of your life?

_____

_____

Questions for Group Discussion

1. The definition of beauty varies from culture to culture. One nation's beauty queen may be another's last-place contestant. Who sets the standard for attractiveness or success in your world?

2. Do you feel pressured to measure up to those standards?

3. The six character qualities that Esther modeled set a different kind of character standard. Take a moment to review the qualities from this chapter. In your opinion, what makes these so attractive and unusual?

4. Imagine yourself in Esther's silk slippers. Every day for twelve months, you're pampered and primped, soaked and sauna-ed, massaged and manicured. Seven maids are at your service with one assignment in mind: to make you more attractive than the other contestants. What sorts of temptations would you battle?

5. Our image-obsessed world can make us feel like we're competing in a kind of beauty contest every day. But really, we should be spending our time making ourselves beautiful, not for a king, but for the King of Kings. What sort of "beauty" treatments are you giving yourself every day to prepare for the moment you come into His presence?

Chapter 4

AN EVIL INTERLUDE

Esther 2:21–3:15

If you were to look up the word *life* in heaven's thesaurus, one of the first synonyms you would find is *pain*.

Life is filled with sharp corners and hard floors. Try as we might to cushion ourselves from the bumps and brace ourselves for the falls, pain is inescapable. It comes with the territory. We can't huddle ourselves away in some cave to avoid it. Neither can we hope that our faith will insulate us from the cold, hard realities of life. It certainly didn't with saints of old.

Innocent Job was covered with skin ulcers, faithful Daniel was thrown into a lions' den, godly Joseph was imprisoned. Courageous Paul was beaten, bold John the Baptizer was beheaded, Spirit-filled Stephen was stoned . . . and even Jesus, the sinless Son of God, was tortured and crucified.

Speaking out of his pain, Job tells us:

> "Man, who is born of woman,
> Is short-lived and full of turmoil." (Job 14:1)

The Living Bible distills his words into three succinct statements: "How frail is man, how few his days, how full of trouble!" Earlier in the book, Job's "comforter" Eliphaz remarks:

> "For man is born for trouble,
> As sparks fly upward." (5:7)

"Born for trouble." Isn't it time we stopped trying to escape the inescapable? Isn't it time we faced up to pain and suffering and hardship and affliction? Isn't it time we stopped skipping class and took our seats to learn the lessons pain has to teach?

Suffering: A Repeated Theme throughout Life

When we analyze life's troubles, the categories seem legion, don't they?

Categories of Suffering

There are disasters in the natural world: earthquakes, tornadoes, hurricanes, floods, mud slides, blizzards, droughts.

There are physical afflictions: injuries, birth defects, handicaps, disabilities, diseases, burns, assaults.

There are emotional traumas: abuses, phobias, depressions, neuroses, self-image struggles.

There are domestic conflicts: husband-and-wife battles, parent-and-child problems, decisions about aging parents, arguments over finances.

Then there are national and international concerns: crime, drugs, gangs, war, pollution, economic worries on a global scale.

Job was right: "How frail is man, how few his days, how full of trouble!" (LB).

Reaction to Suffering

In his book *The Road Less Traveled*, M. Scott Peck echoes what Job said thousands of years earlier.

> What makes life difficult is that the process of confronting and solving problems is a painful one. Problems, depending upon their nature, evoke in us frustration or grief or sadness or loneliness or guilt or regret or anger or fear or anxiety or anguish or despair. These are uncomfortable feelings, often very uncomfortable, often as painful as any kind of physical pain, sometimes equaling the very worst kind of physical pain. Indeed, it is *because* of the pain that events or conflicts engender in us that we call them problems. And since life poses an endless series of problems, life is always difficult and is full of pain as well as joy.[1]

Since pain is so pervasive, how should we react to it? Well, we can never respond correctly to life's hurts unless we have the correct theological understanding of them. At the center of them all is Evil with a capital E. Evil entered the world when humanity morally stumbled and fell in the Garden of Eden (see Gen. 2:16–17; Rom. 5:12).

From that time a Pandora's box remained forever open. Pain, hardship, suffering, sorrow, and death flowed from Paradise Lost to

---

1. M. Scott Peck, *The Road Less Traveled* (New York, N.Y.: Simon and Schuster, A Touchstone Book, 1978), p. 16.

pollute the entire earth (Gen. 3:16–19). No matter how pristine the beauty of Eden had been, it now lay overgrown with thorns and thistles in a state of moral and physical ruin.

All this brings us back to our friend Esther, an unspoiled flower in the King of Persia's garden. Unfortunately, lurking in the shadows and casting its dark pallor over her queenly throne, is evil. With it, this evil brings pain and ultimately death.

Mutiny: A Minor Plot against the King

At this moment in our fairy tale story, we anticipate the idyllic ending, "And they lived happily ever after." But the story takes a turn down a dark alley instead.

Secret Conspiracy

We pick up the story where two of the king's men are plotting from the shadowy recesses of their evil hearts.

> In those days, while Mordecai was sitting at the king's gate, Bigthan and Teresh, two of the king's officials from those who guarded the door, became angry and sought to lay hands on King Ahasuerus. (Esther 2:21)

Bigthan's and Teresh's anger toward the king festered into a plan of murder.

Swift Punishment

Word of the plot leaked out to Mordecai, and from him, through Esther to the king (v. 22). The insurgents were sentenced to death, and before the ink was dry on the decree, they were history.

> Now when the plot was investigated and found to be so, they were both hanged on a gallows; and it was written in the Book of the Chronicles in the king's presence. (v. 23)

The tendency is to think that since evil was decisively dealt with, peace returned to the royal palace. Not so. Evil rears its ugly head again—this time, farther up the official ladder.

Vengeance: A Major Scheme against the Jews

Since Mordecai saved the king's life, you would think he would be first in line for a promotion to prime minister. But he was passed over—just another example that deserving people often get overlooked and that righteousness often goes unrewarded. It's unfair, but that's how life is.

The one who did get the promotion was Haman, an anti-Semite bent on Mordecai's destruction.

> After these events King Ahasuerus promoted Haman, the son of Hammedatha the Agagite, and advanced him and established his authority over all the princes who were with him. All the king's servants who were at the king's gate bowed down and paid homage to Haman; for so the king had commanded concerning him. But Mordecai neither bowed down nor paid homage. Then the king's servants who were at the king's gate said to Mordecai, "Why are you transgressing the king's command?" Now it was when they had spoken daily to him and he would not listen to them, that they told Haman to see whether Mordecai's reason would stand; for he had told them that he was a Jew. When Haman saw that Mordecai neither bowed down nor paid homage to him, Haman was filled with rage. But he disdained to lay hands on Mordecai alone, for they had told him who the people of Mordecai were. (3:1–6a)

The roots of Haman's bitterness toward the Jews can be traced back to his family tree. He was a descendant of Agag, the Amalekite king whom God commanded Saul to destroy. When Saul killed all the Amalekites he could find but spared Agag and kept the cream of the plunder, the prophet Samuel rebuked Saul and killed Agag himself (see 1 Sam. 15:32–33). The surviving Amalekites had remained bitter enemies of the Jews, and the feud was taken up centuries later by Haman. Prejudice is a vicious evil. And it's hereditary, passed down from generation to generation.

When Mordecai refused to bow down, the anti-Semitic hair on the back of Haman's neck stood on end. He became "filled with rage" (Esther 3:5).

Mordecai refused to bow down for two reasons: (1) The act would be considered idolatry by a Jew, and (2) in no way did he want to show respect to an Amalekite, an avowed enemy of his people (see Exod. 17:8–16).[2]

Plan for Extermination

Haman's hatred seethed in a caldron that spilled over not only on Mordecai but on all of Mordecai's people.

> Therefore Haman sought to destroy all the Jews, the people of Mordecai, who were throughout the whole kingdom of Ahasuerus. (Esther 3:6b)

Haman is a prime example of just how deceitful and desperately wicked the human heart can be, for it was from the murky depths of hearts like Haman's that the Holocaust was dredged up (see Jer. 17:9; Rom. 3:12–18). Like the barbwired concentration camps that destroyed the lives of so many Jews during World War II, the racial hatred in Esther's day laid in wait for Jewish blood, threatening the destruction of her entire race.

Haman wasted no time engineering the fate of the Jews. As soon as the date of their doom was superstitiously determined, he went to the king with his plan.

> In the first month, which is the month Nisan, in the twelfth year of King Ahasuerus, Pur, that is the lot, was cast before Haman from day to day and from month to month, until the twelfth month, that is the month Adar. Then Haman said to King Ahasuerus, "There is a certain people scattered and dispersed among the peoples in all the provinces of your kingdom; their laws are different from those of all other people and they do not observe the king's laws, so it is not in the king's interest to let them remain." (Esther 3:7–8)

---

2. "The Amalekites had been Israel's chief enemy during the wilderness wanderings under Moses, when the people of God were in process of formation. It was decreed then that '"The Lord will have war with Amalek from generation to generation"' (Exod. 17:16). They were the enemy who first and most obviously sought to deny Israel entry into the promised land. In Deuteronomy they were denounced for having picked off the stragglers from the Israelite column of march. . . . So they were far more than one among many military enemies—they were the opponents of God's ways." Eugene H. Peterson, *Five Smooth Stones for Pastoral Work* (Grand Rapids, Mich.: William B. Eerdmans Publishing Co., 1980), pp. 217–18.

Haman then sweetened the rotten pot with a spice he hoped would appeal to the king's palate—a pinch of greed.

> "If it is pleasing to the king, let it be decreed that
> they be destroyed, and I will pay ten thousand talents
> of silver into the hands of those who carry on the
> king's business, to put into the king's treasuries." (v. 9)

Ten thousand talents of silver equaled 375 tons, estimated to represent two-thirds of the annual income of the entire Persian Empire. No doubt Haman planned to make good on his pledge by confiscating the assets of those he annihilated.

The plan sounded in the best interests of the empire, so the king gave it a "thumbs up." And he even told Haman he could keep the silver for himself!

> Then the king took his signet ring from his hand
> and gave it to Haman, the son of Hammedatha the
> Agagite, the enemy of the Jews. The king said to
> Haman, "The silver is yours, and the people also, to
> do with them as you please." (vv. 10–11)

Announcement to All

The entire plot had been synchronized like clockwork. The scribes were poised and ready to write. The ring on Haman's hand gave him the power of attorney to set the king's seal on any document he drafted. The couriers were ready to ride their steeds to all the provinces of the kingdom, and the heralds' lips were pursed to cry, "Hear ye! Hear ye!" (vv. 12–13). The gears were set in motion.

> Letters were sent by couriers to all the king's prov-
> inces to destroy, to kill and to annihilate all the
> Jews, both young and old, women and children, in
> one day, the thirteenth day of the twelfth month,
> which is the month Adar, and to seize their posses-
> sions as plunder. A copy of the edict to be issued as
> law in every province was published to all the peo-
> ples so that they should be ready for this day. The
> couriers went out impelled by the king's command
> while the decree was issued at the citadel in Susa;
> and while the king and Haman sat down to drink,
> the city of Susa was in confusion. (vv. 13–15)

The scene in the last verse is ironic—the king and Haman sitting down for a peaceful drink while the city stumbled over itself in bewilderment. Like our Friday the thirteenth, this thirteenth of Adar loomed in the people's minds with a macabre foreboding. In just eleven months the streets would become tributaries of blood, rivers of racial hatred red with anti-Semitism.[3]

Thus falls the curtain on act 2 of our drama. And it doesn't look good for the Jewish people.

Wickedness: An Appropriate Response

Besides the two who were hanged, three male actors have performed in our drama so far: Mordecai, Haman, and King Ahasuerus. Each of these characters has something specific to teach us.

From Mordecai we learn this: *Always remember that someone will resent your independent devotion to the Lord.* Mordecai's loyalty to God prevented him from bowing his knee to Haman the prime minister. Our devotion to God should also keep us from compromising our convictions.

From Haman we learn: *Never underestimate the diabolical nature of revenge.* It will poison your life if you do. Proverbs says to "watch over your heart with all diligence, For from it flow the springs of life" (4:23). If the source itself becomes poisoned, so will all the streams that flow from it.

From the king we learn: *Never overestimate your own importance.* Some wise counselor should have come up alongside Ahasuerus and said to him, "What is this you're allowing? And why? Not even you are important enough to decide the fate of an entire nation!"

There have been or will be evil interludes in all of our lives. But we don't have to follow the script wickedness has written. We can break out of that role. We can change that tragic story line. But to do that we have to have Mordecai's convictions keeping us from compromise.

---

3. Until now, the Persians had been supportive of the Jews. King Cyrus had allowed them to return to Jerusalem and even ordered an offering to be collected for restoring the temple (Ezra 1:1–4). Later, King Darius I commanded Israel's enemies to leave the Jews alone so they could finish rebuilding the temple (6:6–12). In stark contrast was King Ahasuerus' edict, which contradicted years of tolerance and came as a complete surprise.

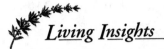

Living Insights

It was Haman who plotted the destruction of the Jews—not God. So we should point the finger of blame not heavenward but heartward, for it was the wickedness in Haman's heart that engendered this great evil. As C. S. Lewis noted:

> When souls become wicked they will certainly use this possibility to hurt one another; and this, perhaps, accounts for four-fifths of the sufferings of men. It is men, not God, who have produced racks, whips, prisons, slavery, guns, bayonets, and bombs.[4]

From world wars to family feuds, from street violence to office backstabbing, all the evil that people inflict on each other flows from the same source: the heart. Realizing his sinful potential, David asked for the Lord's light to penetrate his mind:

> Search me, O God, and know my heart;
> Try me and know my anxious thoughts;
> And see if there be any hurtful way in me,
> And lead me in the everlasting way.
> (Ps. 139:23–24)

Is God revealing any "hurtful way" in you? Perhaps subconsciously, have you been plotting someone's downfall? Have you been thrusting any bayonets of sarcasm or hurling bombs of criticism behind anyone's back?

_____

_____

What sinful motive could be fueling your actions? An injured ego? An insatiable jealousy?

_____

_____

4. C. S. Lewis, *The Problem of Pain* (reprint; New York, N.Y.: Macmillan Publishing Co., Collier Books, 1962), p. 89.

Are you prepared to make things right with this person? What do you need to say or do?

_____

_____

The way of revenge is a broad and slippery road that often leads to our downfall. The narrow way of honesty and forgiveness is steep but at the end is life and freedom.

Which path are you taking? If you're headed the wrong way, just remember, God allows U-turns (see Ps. 51:10; Acts 3:19).

 *Questions for Group Discussion*

1. After Mordecai reveals the conspiracy and saves Ahasuerus' life, we expect to read of his promotion. Instead, what do we read in Esther 3:1? What thoughts do you think may have been going through Mordecai's mind?

2. How do you respond when a Haman-type person gets promoted ahead of you?

3. What does 1 Peter 5:6–7 say to do? Is this a hard command for you to obey?

4. As the arrogant and conniving Haman sauntered into the palace, do you think Esther and Mordecai questioned God's providence? What doubts may have surfaced?

5. Esther and Mordecai couldn't turn to the final chapter of their story and read how everything turned out, and neither can we when it comes to our life story. But we do know the author, and we know that He "causes all things to work together for good to those who love God, to those who are called according to His purpose" (Rom. 8:28). Are you battling doubts right now? In what situation do you need to trust God's ways even though you don't understand them?

Chapter 5

THINKING AND SAYING WHAT'S RIGHT—REGARDLESS

Esther 4

In a world of more than five billion people, it's easy to feel lost among the statistics. But you are not a number; you are unique (Ps. 139:13–14). There is no one quite like you in all the world. Even though you may feel insignificant from time to time, your life matters. As author Edward Everett Hale said:

> I am only one.
> But still I am one.
> I cannot do everything,
> But still I can do something;
> And because I cannot do everything
> I will not refuse to do the something that
> I can do.[1]

The Significant Impact of One Person

Both history and Scripture are full of people who thought like Edward Hale—people of conviction, people of courage, people who made a difference.

In History

Who can possibly measure the unending shadows cast by individuals who stood tall in their own lifetimes? Artists like da Vinci and Michelangelo. Military leaders like Lee, MacArthur, Eisenhower. Statesmen like Washington and Lincoln. Clergymen like Luther, Calvin, Wesley. Heroines like Joan of Arc, Madame Curie, Florence Nightingale, Amelia Earhart, Corrie ten Boom.

Of course, it may be argued that these were incredibly courageous individuals, some gifted, geniuses, or people who held positions of high rank. And you may be thinking, "What about little old me? What difference can I make?"

---

1. Edward Everett Hale, as quoted in *Bartlett's Familiar Quotations*, 15th ed., rev. and enl., ed. Emily Morison Beck (Boston, Mass.: Little, Brown and Co., 1980), p. 590.

But one ordinary person can make a big difference. Just look at these examples.

> In 1776, One vote gave America the English
>   language instead of German; . . .
> In 1845, One vote brought Texas into the Union;
> In 1868, One vote saved President Andrew
>   Johnson from impeachment; . . .
> In 1876, One vote gave Rutherford B. Hayes
>   the U.S. Presidency;
> In 1923, One vote gave Adolph Hitler control
>   of the Nazi Party.[2]

In Scripture

The Bible is not a book that simply chronicles sweeping crusades or mass movements. It is also the story of individuals—people like us. Ordinary people who decided to do something, to make a contribution, to stand up and be counted.

God, much more so than the Marines, is looking for a few good men—and women.

> "For the eyes of the Lord move to and fro throughout the earth that He may strongly support those whose heart is completely His." (2 Chron. 16:9a)

> "I searched for a man among them who would build up the wall and stand in the gap before Me for the land, so that I would not destroy it; but I found no one." (Ezek. 22:30)

> They forgot God their Savior,
> Who had done great things in Egypt,
> Wonders in the land of Ham
> And awesome things by the Red Sea.
> Therefore He said that He would destroy them,
> Had not Moses His chosen one stood in the
>   breach before Him,
> To turn away His wrath from destroying them.
> (Ps. 106:21–23)

---

2. "One Vote," quoted by John Salisbury in "A Message for Americans," on KXL [Radio], Portland, Oregon. Courtesy of the Multnomah County Republican Central Committee, April 1978. See also Paul Lee Tan, comp., *Encyclopedia of 7,700 Illustrations: Signs of the Times* (Assurance Publishers, 1979), p. 620.

In the last passage, we see that Moses' intercession turned God's wrath away from destroying a rebellious generation. In this chapter from Esther, her intercession will be crucial in saving her generation too.

The Essential Intercession of Queen Esther

For Esther's people in Persia, life turned bleak overnight. Because of a wicked plan conceived in the anti-Semitic mind of Haman, every Jew in the nation was suddenly living on borrowed time. Before the year was out, their bodies would lie in the mass graves of genocide, placed there by their Gentile neighbors. We see the diabolical plan set in motion in Esther 3:8–15. The capital city was thrown into a state of confusion. For decades, the Persian policy toward foreigners had been one of toleration. Was this new edict the beginning of hostilities toward all races? The Jews, of course, were particularly stunned by the news. Could the royal edict really be true? Could there be no appeal? Couldn't anyone change the plan? Amend it? Delay it? Abolish it?

For the Jews, the sky was falling, and there was no place to hide.

Mourning and Weeping

The edict devastated the Jews. Every one of them who heard it cried out to God.

> When Mordecai learned all that had been done, he tore his clothes, put on sackcloth and ashes, and went out into the midst of the city and wailed loudly and bitterly. He went as far as the king's gate, for no one was to enter the king's gate clothed in sackcloth. In each and every province where the command and decree of the king came, there was great mourning among the Jews, with fasting, weeping and wailing; and many lay on sackcloth and ashes. (4:1–3)

To this day people of Eastern cultures do not restrain their grief. Funeral processions are public times of loud wailing and weeping. No one hides their sorrow at tragic events, and Mordecai didn't either.

It was common in those days to wear loose-fitting, dark-colored, coarsely-woven garments made of goat's hair to signify repentance; sitting in a pile of ashes was a way of showing bitter remorse. So for Mordecai and the other Jews, doing these things was an acknowledgment that they were in utter ruin and that only God could restore them.

Esther, however, lived in another world, a world of silks and satins, sheltered from the sorrow in the street. That is, until news of her people's mourning reached her.

> Then Esther's maidens and her eunuchs came and told her, and the queen writhed in great anguish. (v. 4a)

Informing and Responding

Seeking a reliable source to explain this outburst of sorrow among her people, Esther sent a servant to question her cousin Mordecai.

> And she sent garments to clothe Mordecai that he might remove his sackcloth from him, but he did not accept them. Then Esther summoned Hathach from the king's eunuchs, whom the king had appointed to attend her, and ordered him to go to Mordecai to learn what this was and why it was. So Hathach went out to Mordecai to the city square in front of the king's gate. Mordecai told him all that had happened to him, and the exact amount of money that Haman had promised to pay to the king's treasuries for the destruction of the Jews. He also gave him a copy of the text of the edict which had been issued in Susa for their destruction. (vv. 4b–8a)

In the verses, notice the following phrases: "*all* that happened" . . . "*exact* amount of money" . . . "a *copy* of the text of the edict." See how carefully Mordecai passed on the information to Esther? He didn't hide the truth, but neither did he exaggerate. He didn't estimate numbers; he was exact. He didn't pass on rumors; he provided her with documented information.

Let's pause here for a moment of application. Are you that careful in passing along information? Are you able to document your stories? Do you make sure of the facts you're communicating?

Mordecai was careful to pass on accurate facts because he wanted the queen to be well-informed. And he wanted her to be well-informed because he wanted her to get involved. In fact, through Hathach he ordered her "to go in to the king to implore his favor and to plead with him for her people" (v. 8b).

Undergirding Mordecai's plea for Esther's involvement was the belief that one person can make a difference. But Esther churned at the request. Yes, there were her people to think about, but there was also her own life.

> Then Esther spoke to Hathach and ordered him to reply to Mordecai: "All the king's servants and the people of the king's provinces know that for any man or woman who comes to the king to the inner court who is not summoned, he has but one law, that he be put to death, unless the king holds out to him the golden scepter so that he may live. And I have not been summoned to come to the king for these thirty days." They related Esther's words to Mordecai. (vv. 10–12)

Pleading and Praying

Upon hearing her response, Mordecai was faced with a dilemma. Should he back off or add pressure? With parental frankness, he sent a second appeal.

> Then Mordecai told them to reply to Esther, "Do not imagine that you in the king's palace can escape any more than all the Jews. For if you remain silent at this time, relief and deliverance will arise for the Jews from another place and you and your father's house will perish. And who knows whether you have not attained royalty for such a time as this?" (vv. 13–14)

Follow the lines of his reasoning: First, if you do nothing, sooner or later they will find out that you are a Jew and you, too, will be destroyed. Second, the Jewish race *will* survive, for God's promise to His people is greater than your willingness to be involved—if He has to, God will simply use someone else (see Gen. 12:1–3). Third, this threat to God's people could explain why you were elevated to such a high position.

Mordecai's power-packed rhetoric is reminiscent of one of the fiery speeches of Winston Churchill: "Let us . . . brace ourselves to our duties, and so bear ourselves that if the British Empire and its Commonwealth last for a thousand years, men will still say: 'This was their finest hour.'"[3]

3. Sir Winston Churchill, as quoted in *Bartlett's Familiar Quotations*, p. 744.

Esther had the same opportunity the British people had during World War II. If she chose to stand, this could be her finest hour. Her decision? It's found in the very next verses.

> Then Esther told them to reply to Mordecai, "Go, assemble all the Jews who are found in Susa, and fast for me; do not eat or drink for three days, night or day. I and my maidens also will fast in the same way. And thus I will go in to the king, which is not according to the law; and if I perish, I perish." (Esther 4:15–16)

The king had chosen her to be queen on the basis of her beauty; God had chosen her on the basis of her character. And now her character was rising to the occasion with heroic resolve: "If I perish, I perish." And not only did Esther rise to heroism but to leadership as well.

> So Mordecai went away and did just as Esther had commanded him. (v. 17)

Notice how Esther's entire outlook shifted in the space of this chapter. From fear to faith. From reluctance to resolve. From concern for her personal safety to the concern for the safety of her people. And from respect for Mordecai's leadership to the emergence of her own.

The Personal Involvement of Each Individual

As our world becomes more and more crowded, it's easy to feel lost in that crowd or to underestimate our significance. We wonder what difference we could possibly make in light of the spread of problems as abortion, homelessness, crime, hunger, and drugs.

But one person *can* make a difference. Look at Mother Teresa or Billy Graham. Not until we believe this is true will we really be willing to risk. And only when we move from the safe harbor of theory to the rough waters of reality—to actually *do* something— will we see any changes take place.

Do you really want to know how much difference one person can make? Scripture tells us that Jesus values one person so much that He's willing to leave the ninety-nine sheep that are safe and go after the one that is lost (see Luke 15:3–7). For no matter how big the fold, *one* is always a valuable number to God.

Living Insights

Consider the life of one person who made a significant difference in the world, as described by one of her contemporaries.

> She is the most revered woman in the world. Mother Teresa's work among the dying on the streets of Calcutta is legendary. . . . Recipient of the Nobel Peace Prize for her world impact for good, Mother Teresa is an eloquent example of Christlike compassion.
>
> Her indelible impact on the one-time enfant terrible of journalism, Malcolm Muggeridge, is recorded in his book, *Something Beautiful for God:* "In a dark time she is a burning and a shining light; in a cruel time, a living embodiment of Christ's gospel of love; in a godless time, the Word dwelling among us, full of grace and truth . . . All who have had the inestimable privilege of knowing her must be eternally grateful.". . .
>
> "I am like a little pencil in His hand" she says of her ministry. "That is all. He does the thinking. He does the writing. The pencil has nothing to do with it. The pencil has only to be allowed to be used."[4]

Consider one more solitary life—yours. What beautiful stories God could write if only you placed that little pencil in His hand. Won't you pray along with the following petition from Saint Francis of Assisi and yield your life to Him?

> Lord, make me an instrument of Your peace.
> Where there is hatred, let me sow love;
> Where there is injury, pardon;
> Where there is doubt, faith;
> Where there is despair, hope;
> Where there is darkness, light;
> And where there is sadness, joy.
>
> O Divine Master, grant that I may not
> So much seek to be consoled as to console;

4. "Something Beautiful for God," *The War Cry,* March 3, 1990, p. 2.

To be understood as to understand;
To be loved as to love;
For it is in giving that we receive;
It is in pardoning that we are pardoned;
And it is in dying
That we are born to eternal life.[5]

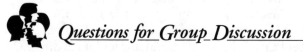 *Questions for Group Discussion*

1. Haman, the antagonist in the story, is one example of how Satan uses earthly powers to destroy God's people and obstruct His ways. Who are some of the "Hamans" who threaten you, your church, Christendom, or the world at large?

2. Prior to World War II, Hitler's Nazi threat forced the nations of the world to rethink their priorities and link arms in the cause of freedom. In a similar sense, Haman's threat forced Esther to rearrange her priorities and join her people in the cause of God. How does realizing you have an "enemy" change your priorities? What is less important? What is more important?

3. Mordecai's appeal to Esther in 4:14 maintains a perfect balance between God's sovereignty in the crisis and Esther's responsibility. Can you identify both themes in this verse?

4. What did Esther have to lose by revealing her true identity to the king? What did she have to gain?

5. What do you have to lose by revealing your identity as a Christian and standing up for the cause of Christ? What do you have to gain?

6. What was Esther's attitude in verse 16? How does her response to Mordecai inspire you in your situation?

5. Saint Francis of Assisi, as quoted in *Every Knee Shall Bow*, comp. and ed. Joan Winmill Brown (Minneapolis, Minn.: Grason, 1978), p. 20.

Chapter 6
ESTHER'S FINEST HOUR
Esther 5

Martin Luther took a stand against the most formidable power of his time—the Roman Catholic Church. He was like the Little Engine That Could going up against the entire Union Pacific Railroad.

In 1517 Luther called for a debate by nailing his Ninety-Five Theses on the Castle Church door in Wittenberg. This debate, along with his lectures and books, put him on a track that ran to Rome. A collision was inevitable.

In April of 1521 the governing council of the Germanic states convened in the city of Worms to confront Luther about his beliefs. When asked if he would renounce his inflammatory statements about the pope and the church, he faced his accusers with stalwart resolve and proclaimed:

> Unless I am convicted by Scripture and plain reason— I do not accept the authority of popes and councils, for they have contradicted each other—my conscience is captive to the Word of God. I cannot and I will not recant anything, for to go against conscience is neither right nor safe. Here I stand. I cannot do otherwise. God help me. Amen.[1]

We saw this same type of resolve in Esther when she decided to go alone before the most powerful man in Medo-Persia—her husband, the king.

> "And thus I will go in to the king, which is not according to the law; and if I perish, I perish." (Esther 4:16b)

Such courage is what cements our convictions so that we, like Luther and Esther, can stand up for what's right, even when we have to stand alone.

---

1. Martin Luther, as quoted in *Here I Stand*, by Roland H. Bainton (New York, N.Y.: New American Library of World Literature, Mentor Books, 1950), pp. 144–45.

A Silent yet Powerful Interlude

Upon Mordecai's challenge, Esther didn't race immediately into the king's presence. Wisely, she waited, making a request of Mordecai first.

> "Go, assemble all the Jews who are found in Susa,
> and fast for me; do not eat or drink for three days,
> night or day." (v. 16a)

Mordecai obeyed Esther's command (v. 17); for three days the Jewish people fasted. During this time they calmed their emotions, gained perspective, and placed their problem in the hands of God— just as the prophet Isaiah advises in his book.

> Yet those who wait for the Lord
> Will gain new strength;
> They will mount up with wings like eagles,
> They will run and not get tired,
> They will walk and not become weary. (Isa. 40:31)

From this verse we learn of four things that happen when we wait on God rather than rush into a frenzy of activity. First, *we gain new strength*—which we'll need when the road gets rocky. Second, *we get a better perspective*—which gives us an eagle's-eye view of our circumstances. Third, *we store up extra energy*—which we can draw upon at a later time. Fourth, *we deepen our determination to persevere*— which wards off weariness.

When we wait on the Lord, in addition to gaining new strength we step aside to make room for His awesome work on our behalf.

> "'Do not fear, for I am with you;
> Do not anxiously look about you, for I am your God.
> I will strengthen you, surely I will help you,
> Surely I will uphold you with My righteous
> right hand.'
> Behold, all those who are angered at you will be
> shamed and dishonored;
> Those who contend with you will be as nothing
> and will perish.
> You will seek those who quarrel with you, but
> will not find them,
> Those who war with you will be as nothing and
> non-existent.

For I am the Lord your God, who upholds your
    right hand,
Who says to you, 'Do not fear, I will help you.'"
(41:10–13)

Undoubtedly, these benefits of waiting strengthened Esther's resolve during her three-day fast. It was a silent yet powerful interlude in the queen's life.

Calm yet Wise Plan

For three days Esther has waited on the Lord. Now it is time to test her eagle's wings.

> Now it came about on the third day that Esther put on her royal robes and stood in the inner court of the king's palace in front of the king's rooms, and the king was sitting on his royal throne in the throne room, opposite the entrance to the palace. When the king saw Esther the queen standing in the court, she obtained favor in his sight; and the king extended to Esther the golden scepter which was in his hand. So Esther came near and touched the top of the scepter. Then the king said to her, "What is troubling you, Queen Esther? And what is your request? Even to half of the kingdom it shall be given to you." (Esther 5:1–3)

During times of prayer, fasting, and waiting, God prepares not only our hearts but the hearts of those with whom we could have conflict—even those who might be unpredictable or hostile. See how softened the king's heart is toward Esther. In verse 2, "she obtained favor in his sight." In verse 3, he asked, "What is troubling you?"

Calmly, Esther unfolds the first step of her plan.

> Esther said, "If it please the king, may the king and Haman come this day to the banquet that I have prepared for him." (v. 4)

Notice Esther's self-control. She doesn't spill out what's troubling her. She doesn't point a finger at Haman and ask for his head. She doesn't play on the king's emotions and manipulate him into action. She doesn't get into a frenzy or act in haste. Instead, she restrains herself and stays with her prayed-over plan: issuing the king an invitation.

Notice also that she has readied the banquet for that day. But wait—when would she have had time to prepare for such a party? During her three days of fasting. You see, waiting on the Lord doesn't mean we become inert. We listen for His leading and plan and prepare accordingly.

With the table set and the invitation accepted, the issue of Esther's request comes up again.

> Then the king said, "Bring Haman quickly that we may do as Esther desires." So the king and Haman came to the banquet which Esther had prepared. As they drank their wine at the banquet, the king said to Esther, "What is your petition, for it shall be granted to you. And what is your request? Even to half of the kingdom it shall be done." So Esther replied, "My petition and my request is: if I have found favor in the sight of the king, and if it pleases the king to grant my petition and do what I request, may the king and Haman come to the banquet which I shall prepare for them, and tomorrow I will do as the king says." (vv. 5–8)

Instead of answering the king's question, Esther invites him and Haman to still another banquet. Here the queen is a perfect example of peace and patience. She doesn't panic, because her confidence is not her own. Her waiting has produced in her a greater sensitivity to God, who probably helped her know that the time for answering the king was just not yet.

A Proud and Sinister Response

In verse 9, the spotlight of the story turns suddenly onto Haman. Watch his arrogance turn into rage in the following verses.

> Then Haman went out that day glad and pleased of heart; but when Haman saw Mordecai in the king's gate and that he did not stand up or tremble before him, Haman was filled with anger against Mordecai. Haman controlled himself, however, went to his house and sent for his friends and his wife Zeresh. Then Haman recounted to them the

glory of his riches, and the number of his sons, and every instance where the king had magnified him and how he had promoted him above the princes and servants of the king. Haman also said, "Even Esther the queen let no one but me come with the king to the banquet which she had prepared; and tomorrow also I am invited by her with the king." (vv. 9–12)

What pride! He stands there preening himself, like a peacock spreading its iridescent feathers for all to admire. When a person is this self-absorbed, he focuses not on all those who venerate him but on the one who refuses to. That's why Mordecai grated on Haman so.

"Yet all of this does not satisfy me every time I see Mordecai the Jew sitting at the king's gate." (v. 13)

Seeing how flustered Haman was, his wife and friends came up with a solution that would keep Mordecai from spoiling his next dinner with the king.

Then Zeresh his wife and all his friends said to him, "Have a gallows fifty cubits high made and in the morning ask the king to have Mordecai hanged on it; then go joyfully with the king to the banquet." And the advice pleased Haman, so he had the gallows made.[2] (v. 14)

Some Direct and Timely Advice

Woven into the fabric of our story today are four threads of advice. Let's unravel them one by one and knit them into our lives.

First, *when preparing for an unprecedented event, wait on the Lord before getting involved.* At least as important as what we wait for is the work God does—in us, in others, in our circumstances—while we wait.

---

2. We think of gallows as a structure designed to hang someone by the neck, but the Persians used gallows for a much crueler form of execution. "Among the Persians this form of execution was impalement, as is confirmed in pictures and statues from the ancient Near East." Raymond Dillard and Edwin Yamauchi, footnote on Esther 2:23, in *The NIV Study Bible*, ed. Kenneth Barker and others (Grand Rapids, Mich.: Zondervan Bible Publishers, 1985), p. 722.

Second, *when dealing with an unpredictable person, count on the Lord to open the doors.* Amazing things happen to our courage while we're waiting. Instead of becoming more afraid of our enemy, we become more confident in God.

Third, *when working through an unpleasant situation, trust the Lord for enduring patience.* In situations that are unpleasant, timing is as important as actions—sometimes more so. Pace yourself. It takes patience for the situation to become bearable and workable.

Fourth, *when standing against an unprincipled enemy, ask the Lord for invincible courage.* God gave Esther the nerve to step into the king's presence uninvited; He gave Martin Luther the backbone to stand against the most powerful people of his day; and He can give you the grit you need to hold fast to what you believe.

Our lesson today ends like the cliff-hangers of the old-time serials on the silent screen. Mordecai is about to be tied to the railroad track. Only Esther can save him. But will she rescue him in time? Will she thwart Haman's insidious plot to rid the empire of the Jewish people? At the risk of being melodramatic, all we can say is, "Tune in next time!"

Living Insights

Let's personalize the advice found at the end of our lesson.

Are you facing an unprecedented event in your life? Are you at a critical juncture where you need to decide or act or speak? If you are, try waiting on God before you do. List the possible benefits of including the Lord in your decision making.

_____

_____

_____

Look up the following verses on waiting: Psalm 27:13–14; 62:5; 147:11; Isaiah 26:8; Lamentations 3:25–26. Copy the verse that is most helpful to you in your present circumstances.

_____

_____

_____

Are you presently dealing with an unpredictable person? Here are some verses that may help you count on the Lord to open hearts and doors: Psalm 27:1–3; Proverbs 16:7; 21:1; Matthew 10:29–33. Copy the passage that helps you the most.

_____

_____

_____

Are you working through an unpleasant situation? Are you having difficulty trusting the Lord for patience? If so, maybe these verses will help: Job 23:10; Romans 5:3–5; James 1:2–4; 1 Peter 4:12–19. Of those, copy the one that most helps you to trust God.

_____

_____

_____

Are you standing against an unprincipled enemy? Are your knees knocking for fear of what might happen to you? What you need is courage. See if these verses don't help: 1 Samuel 17:45; 2 Kings 6:15–17; Psalm 18:1–3; Romans 8:31–39. Copy the passage that most strengthens your heart.

_____

_____

_____

_____

_____

_____

Questions for Group Discussion

1. Have you ever been in a situation that felt hopeless? Perhaps things went from bad to worse until a kind of gallows loomed ominously over your life.

2. Was it hard to pray? To wait on the Lord? To keep your faith?

3. Esther's story began hopefully with her becoming queen, but, like the moon's shadow during a solar eclipse, evil slowly passed across her situation until it had blotted out all light and hope. What can you do to keep from panicking while you wait for the darkness to pass and God's light to reemerge?

4. What good comes while you wait on the Lord (see Isa. 40:31; 41:10–13)?

5. What lessons about God can be learned better during times of trouble?

6. Based on her approach to the darkness in her life, what advice do you think Esther would give to help you through your dark periods?

Chapter 7

WHAT GOES AROUND, COMES AROUND

Esther 6

Things are not always as they seem. Here's a case in point.

A shipwrecked man was once washed ashore on an uninhabited island. In the days that followed he painstakingly constructed a hut with a few things he salvaged from the wreck and from whatever he could find on the island. That little hut was the only protection he had from the harsh elements and the only place he could safeguard his meager possessions.

Upon returning one evening from a lengthy search for food, he was terrified to find the hut engulfed in flames. The loss devastated him. He spent that night despondent, sleeping on the sand.

He awoke early the next morning and, to his surprise, saw a ship anchored off the island. A crew member stepped ashore and told him, "We saw your smoke signal and came to rescue you!"[1]

What seemed to be destruction turned out to be deliverance. And such was the case with Mordecai. He had been shipwrecked by an anti-Semitic undercurrent on an island of injustice, and now he stood in death's shadow. Every hope that sheltered him seemed to have gone up in smoke.

But then, as we will find out today, things are not always as they seem.

When All Seems Lost, It Isn't

For the Jews living in Persia in Mordecai's time, it seemed as if all was lost. First, their protection seemed lost. They had no advocate except for the queen. But how powerful was she in the shadow of the king? Second, their future seemed lost. The sand in the hourglass was rapidly running out. Genocide seemed inevitable. As a result, their hope seemed lost.

---

1. This story is adapted from the "Western Recorder," as quoted in the *Encyclopedia of 7,700 Illustrations: Signs of the Times*, comp. Paul Lee Tan (Assurance Publishers, 1979), p. 1516.

Yet in spite of the way things seemed, that's not the way things were. Behind the scenes God was at work. His providential plan to deliver the Jews was being enacted by Esther. The king had given her not only an audience but also carte blanche to request anything she desired, up to half his kingdom.

None of the Jews, though, knew what was happening behind the palace doors. Not even Haman knew. He was too busy building the gallows for his nemesis Mordecai to know anything but his own desire for revenge.

A seven-story gallows couldn't be built in secret. A crowd of curious onlookers must have gathered, and it wasn't long before word spread that Mordecai was the intended victim. How Mordecai must have brooded as the pole for his execution was raised. How ominously it stood, like a cruel scepter raised in judgment over his life.

It would have been easy for Mordecai to curl up and lick his wounds, to bemoan the fact that no one noticed how he had once saved the king but was now being treated unjustly.

This brings us to the second principle.

When No One Seems to Notice, God Does

Just when the shadow of death seemed darkest, a ray of hope shone from the king's chambers.

> During that night the king could not sleep so he gave an order to bring the book of records, the chronicles, and they were read before the king. It was found written what Mordecai had reported concerning Bigthana and Teresh, two of the king's eunuchs who were doorkeepers, that they had sought to lay hands on King Ahasuerus. And the king said, "What honor or dignity has been bestowed on Mordecai for this?" Then the king's servants who attended him said, "Nothing has been done for him." (Esther 6:1–3)

Often, momentous events hang upon the slenderest of threads. Here the deliverance of the Jews was precipitated by something as insignificant as insomnia. While all of Susa slept, the king lay awake—a reminder that God is not distant or indifferent. He sees. He cares. He intervenes on our behalf.

While the king tossed and turned, Mordecai slept. Another

reminder—that God watches over His beloved even while they sleep (Ps. 127:2). So in spite of the fact that no one seemed to notice, God did. That's as true in our day as it was in Mordecai's. Though we may feel abandoned, we are never out of God's watchful eye or far from His protective care.

As a soporific to help him sleep, the king ordered his staff to read to him from the palace chronicles. But in their reading, he found himself suddenly alert instead of slowly anesthetized. The reason was the story of an aborted assassination plot, foiled by . . . Mordecai. Remember the incident?

> In those days, while Mordecai was sitting at the king's gate, Bigthan and Teresh, two of the king's officials from those who guarded the door, became angry and sought to lay hands on King Ahasuerus. But the plot became known to Mordecai and he told Queen Esther, and Esther informed the king in Mordecai's name. Now when the plot was investigated and found to be so, they were both hanged on a gallows; and it was written in the Book of the Chronicles in the king's presence. (Esther 2:21–23)

The king, however, had overlooked Mordecai and found reason to honor Haman (3:1). When people fail to take proper notice, however, remember that God does (see Matt. 6:3–4; Heb. 6:10).

And this brings us to our next principle.

When Everything Seems Great for Our Enemies, It's Not

As soon as the king heard that nothing had been done to reward Mordecai, he immediately set out to rectify the situation. And he sought advice, ironically, from the person whose agenda for Mordecai was diametrically opposed to his.

> So the king said, "Who is in the court?" Now Haman had just entered the outer court of the king's palace in order to speak to the king about hanging Mordecai on the gallows which he had prepared for him. The king's servants said to him, "Behold, Haman is standing in the court." And the king said, "Let him come in." So Haman came in and the king said to him, "What is to be done for the man whom the king desires to honor?" (Esther 6:4–6a)

The king's question started the wheels turning in Haman's greedy mind.

> And Haman said to himself, "Whom would the king desire to honor more than me?" Then Haman said to the king, "For the man whom the king desires to honor, let them bring a royal robe which the king has worn, and the horse on which the king has ridden, and on whose head a royal crown has been placed; and let the robe and the horse be handed over to one of the king's most noble princes and let them array the man whom the king desires to honor and lead him on horseback through the city square, and proclaim before him, 'Thus it shall be done to the man whom the king desires to honor.'" (vv. 6b–9)

Boy, was Haman in for a surprise! You could almost hear his jaw hit the floor when the king unveiled the person of honor.

> Then the king said to Haman, "Take quickly the robes and the horse as you have said, and do so for Mordecai the Jew, who is sitting at the king's gate; do not fall short in anything of all that you have said." (v. 10)

How ironic—the very man champing to hang Mordecai was the one chosen to honor him.

> So Haman took the robe and the horse, and arrayed Mordecai, and led him on horseback through the city square, and proclaimed before him, "Thus it shall be done to the man whom the king desires to honor." (v. 11)

Two more contrasting characters than these could not be placed alongside one another. One sat upon a regal horse, robed in the king's own attire. The other walked before him, proclaiming his praise. The words must have lodged in Haman's throat. How humiliated he must have felt—and how infuriated.

Yet Mordecai remained unaffected by all the pomp and praise. How do we know this? Look at the next verse.

> Then Mordecai returned to the king's gate. (v. 12a)

Where do we find Mordecai, when all the laudatory dust settles?

Back where he started—at the king's gate.

> A proud ambitious man would have said to himself,
> "No more of the king's gate for me! I shall direct
> my steps now to the king's palace, and hold myself
> ready for honour . . . which surely must now be at
> hand." Mordecai seems to have said with himself,
> "*If* these things are designed for me in God's good
> providence, they will find me. But they must seek
> me, for I shall not seek them. Those who confer
> them know my address. 'Mordecai, at the king's
> gate,' will still find me. Let the crowd wonder and
> disperse. I have had enough of their incense. Let
> Haman go whither he will, he is in the hands of the
> Lord. Let my friends at home wait; they will hear
> all in time. . . . I can wait best at the old place
> and in the accustomed way—'*at the king's gate.*'"[2]

When Nothing Seems Just, It Is

It has been said that "the mills of God grind slowly, yet they grind exceedingly small."[3] Haman found himself to be but tiny grist in those mills. His life was under judgment, and it was just a matter of time before the mills of providence would grind his bones to dust.

No longer preening like a peacock, Haman slinked home like a whipped dog, his tail tucked between his legs. He was a beaten man.

> But Haman hurried home, mourning, with his head
> covered. Haman recounted to Zeresh his wife and
> all his friends everything that had happened to him.
> Then his wise men and Zeresh his wife said to him,
> "If Mordecai, before whom you have begun to fall,
> is of Jewish origin, you will not overcome him, but
> will surely fall before him." (vv. 12b–13)

The warning from Haman's wife and wise men comes forth from Scripture like a muted echo from Genesis 12:2–3, where God said

---

2. Alexander Raleigh, *Book of Esther* (1880; reprint, Minneapolis, Minn.: Klock and Klock Christian Publishers, 1980), pp. 155–56.

3. Henry Wadsworth Longfellow, quoted in *The Home Book of Quotations*, 10th ed., comp. Burton Stevenson (New York, N.Y.: Dodd, Mead and Co., 1967), p. 1708.

to Abraham:

> "And I will make you a great nation,
> And I will bless you, . . .
> And I will bless those who bless you,
> *And the one who curses you I will curse.*"
> (emphasis added)

Then, almost before their words could sink in, Haman was whisked off to the royal banquet. Doubtless, his head spun as he ascended the palace steps.

> While they were still talking with him, the king's eunuchs arrived and hastily brought Haman to the banquet which Esther had prepared. (Esther 6:14)

We would have told Haman as he went to the banquet, What goes around comes around. For little did he know that the fateful course he had planned to cater for Mordecai was about to be dished out to him instead.

In Conclusion

We have seen four facets of our lesson's principle: Things are not always as they seem.

- When all seems lost, it isn't.

- When no one seems to notice, God does.

- When everything seems great for our enemies, it's not.

- When nothing seems just, it is.

All this is a long way of saying that even when God seems absent, He is there. In sickness or health. In poverty or prosperity. In promotion or demotion. In the darkest night or the brightest day. He is there, watching, waiting, and working at the slow but sure mills of providence, grinding out His will both upon the wheat and upon the chaff . . . upon the Mordecais as well as the Hamans of this world.

Living Insights

During the arrest, trial, and crucifixion of Christ, things were not as they seemed. It seemed as if Jesus was on His way to defeat. In reality, He was on His way to victory. All appeared dark and hopeless when the cross was shrouded in darkness. But on that first Easter morning, hope dawned triumphantly to herald a risen Savior.

When all seemed lost for the world enslaved in sin, it wasn't.

When no one seemed to notice Christ's agony on the cross, God did.

When everything seemed great for the flaming forces of hell, it wasn't.

When nothing seemed just, justice triumphed in the end.

It's important to understand that if we live our lives by the way things appear, we are living by sight rather than by faith (see 2 Cor. 5:7).

What would have happened to the Jewish race if Esther and Mordecai had lived by sight? What would have happened to the human race if Christ had lived that way? A little closer to home, what would happen to you if you simply lived by the way things appeared?

Have appearances been displaying a deceptive front in your life? Does it seem that all is lost? That no one notices your efforts? That everything is weighted in favor of the ungodly? That justice no longer exists in the world?

Remember the story of Esther and, more importantly, the story of the Cross.

And cling to the promise that things are not always as they seem.

Questions for Group Discussion

1. When Mordecai revealed the assassination plot, his only reward was the satisfaction that he had done the right thing (see Prov. 24:21–22). Little did he know that God would later use his act of saving the king's life to save his own life. Do you sometimes wonder if it is worth it to do the right thing, particularly when you know that no one will notice?

2. What principles do the following verses teach about doing the right thing: Proverbs 19:17; Luke 6:35–38; Hebrews 6:10?

3. How does Haman's life illustrate the proverb, "Pride goes before destruction, And a haughty spirit before stumbling" (Prov. 16:18). Since pride attacks all of us, think of a way you've been attacked and that you feel comfortable sharing with the group.

4. Watching the news on television, we sometimes feel like the prophet Habakkuk, who cried out in dismay, "The law is paralyzed, and justice never prevails" (Hab. 1:4a NIV). What encouragement about God's justice can you glean from Esther's story? What red flags does it raise?

5. When Haman erected the gallows, all seemed lost for Mordecai and the Jews . . . but it wasn't. When the Romans lifted the cross with Jesus on it, all seemed lost for the world . . . but it wasn't. What seems "lost" in your life? What hope can you draw personally from the statement, "With God, things aren't always as they seem"?

Chapter 8

GOD'S SURPRISING SOVEREIGNTY

Esther 7

Poetic justice is "a term introduced into England by Thomas Rymer in 1678, denoting the reward of the virtuous and the punishment of the vicious. . . . Its idea [is] that all characters reap the harvest of their just deserts."[1]

As Christians, we believe that ultimate poetic justice will be meted out at the judgment seat of Christ (2 Cor. 5:10). Until that time, however, we must live with injustice and the silence of heaven's gavel.

Job is a perfect example of someone who not only lived with injustice but wrestled with it. Though godly in heart and righteous in life, Job became the object of Satan's cruelty.

Like a large cat with a tiny, wounded mouse, Satan played havoc with the man, leaving him impoverished, bereaved, and hurting. But the presence of pain was not the hardest part of Job's trial; instead, it was the silence of God.

It was as if God had turned His back on His faithful friend, refusing to look as Job suffered.

It must have been like swimming in a large lake at dusk when a thick fog rolls in. Within seconds, you can see nothing—no horizon, no landmarks, no lights along the shore. You lose all sense of direction. You panic and start swimming in one direction. Then you turn to swim in another. Finally, with your heart pounding, you realize the only thing to do is to tread water and wait for a voice from the shore to orient you.

Undoubtedly, Esther and Mordecai both found themselves enveloped in a fog that muffled the voice of God. All who have suffered the silence of God amidst the presence of injustice can understand their disoriented feelings. The fog is bad enough, but the silence from the shore is unbearable.

Although God is just, He is just in His own time. And in

---

1. Sylvan Barnet, Morton Berman, and William Burto, *A Dictionary of Literary Terms* (1960; reprint, London, England: Constable and Co., 1969), see "poetic justice."

between the ticks of His pocket watch are gaps of silence. Sometimes inexplicable silence.

Understanding God's Timing in Our Day

In order to understand the enigma of God's silence, we have to
understand the difference between our time and God's, between
Earthly Standard Time and Heavenly Mountain Time.

Our Time

Part of trying to reconcile these time zones is understanding
that here on earth we are prisoners of a cage called Time. God
exists outside that cage, unfettered by the constrictions we must
live with, day in, day out.

For us, time is objectively measured. For the day, we look at our
watches. For the week, we turn to our schedules. For the year, we
consult our calendars. Everything we measure is from this present
moment. That is our constant orientation.

For us, time is consciously accountable. Events are seen, visible.
We can even capture them on videotape. The objects involved are
tangible; we can touch them, feel them. And people are present,
witnessing what's said and done.

For us, time is rarely ignored. Only when we sleep or daydream
do we escape from time. Yet even then we cannot escape entirely.
Our jaunt is only mental; physically, we're still captive.

None of the above is true for God. Although we are trapped in
the ever-present Now, God is free from the trammels of time.

God's Time

God's time is *infinitely immeasurable.* And because He transcends
time itself, His time is *absolutely intangible.*

We see history as a sequence of still frames, viewed one after
another, as in a motion picture reel. But God sees the entire movie
at once. That is why He can remain silent in act 1 of the drama
of our lives—because He knows how the final act will turn out.
As author of this epic drama called Life, He knows that ultimately
justice will win out, that good will triumph over evil, and that all
the loose ends will be tied up in His grand denouement.

> No matter how we rationalize, God will sometimes
> *seem* unfair from the perspective of a person trapped
> in time. Only at the end of time, after we have

attained God's level of viewing, after every evil has been punished or forgiven, every illness healed, and the entire universe restored—only then will fairness reign. Then we will understand what role is played by evil, and by the Fall, and by natural law, in an "unfair" event like the death of a child. Until then, we will not know, and can only trust in a God who does know.

We remain ignorant of many details, not because God enjoys keeping us in the dark, but because we have not the faculties to absorb so much light. At a single glance God knows what the world is about and how history will end. But we time-bound creatures have only the most primitive manner of understanding: we can let time pass. Not until history has run its course will we understand how "all things work together for good." Faith means believing in advance what will only make sense in reverse.[2]

Discovering God's Timing in Esther's Day

We love to sing the hymn,

In His time, in His time;
He makes all things beautiful in His time.
Lord, please show me ev'ry day
As You're teaching me Your way,
That You do just what You say in Your time.[3]

Yet the words are harder to sing without divine accompaniment. When there are no notes from heaven to cue us and keep us on key, it's difficult to sing that song. Sure, we can lip-sync the lyrics, but the tune is really not in our hearts, is it?

A Sustained Period of Silence

How difficult it must have been for Esther and Mordecai to sing those stanzas a cappella. When the king promoted Haman, God stayed silent (Esther 3:1). When Haman plotted to destroy the Jews,

2. Philip Yancey, *Disappointment with God* (Grand Rapids, Mich.: Zondervan Publishing House, 1988), pp. 200–201.

3. Diane Ball, "In His Time" (Maranatha! Music, 1978). Administered by The Copyright Company. Used by permission.

God stayed silent (vv. 6–7). When the king made an agreement with Haman, God stayed silent (vv. 8–11). When Mordecai pleaded with the queen to intervene, God stayed silent (chap. 4). When Haman ordered gallows built for Mordecai, God stayed silent (5:14).

The silence of God is deafening in the Book of Esther. But there are other places in Scripture where we strain to hear a word from heaven and hear none.

- The more than four hundred years of silence between the books of Genesis and Exodus.

- The time of Samuel's birth when word from the Lord was rare and visions were infrequent (1 Sam. 3:1).

- The frustrating silence that Habakkuk had to endure (Hab. 1:2–4).

- The four centuries of silence between the testaments, book-ended by Malachi and Matthew.

- The silence of heaven when Jesus hung on the cross (Mark 15:34).

Maybe you're experiencing a similar enigma: How could God be so silent when I cry out to Him so loudly, so desperately? Why doesn't He answer? Why doesn't He call out from the shore so I can orient myself in the fog that has enveloped me? If you find yourself treading water in that foggy lake, remember: *The periods of God's silence are just as significant as the times He speaks.* It is during such times that the ears of our faith become fine-tuned.

A Subtle Turn of Events

In chapter 6 of Esther, we saw that a subtle but pivotal turn of events had taken place. The king couldn't sleep, so he had his servants read the historical records to him. But instead of curing his insomnia, the reading braced him like a pot of hot coffee. The mention of Mordecai's heroism prompted the king to honor this unsung hero. The irony of it all was that the king appointed Haman, Mordecai's sworn enemy, to herald Mordecai's praise. When Haman returned home from this humiliating parade, he heard a different tune from his wife and friends than the one he had heard before. It was as if one day Haman had come home to a festive dance, while the next, to a funeral dirge.

As we stand back and observe this subtle turn of events, we sense that something more is brewing. Amidst the silence, we sense the deeper stirring of God's surprising sovereignty.

A Sudden Change in Plans

These events in chapter 6 usher us into a second banquet in chapter 7.

> Now the king and Haman came to drink wine with Esther the queen. And the king said to Esther on the second day also as they drank their wine at the banquet, "What is your petition, Queen Esther? It shall be granted you. And what is your request? Even to half of the kingdom it shall be done." (vv. 1–2)

This is the third time the king has asked Esther about her petition (see 5:3, 6). Between the time of the first banquet and this one, God inserted an important parenthesis. He revealed to the king how Mordecai had saved his life, which prompted the king to honor this loyal and courageous man.

The delay between the first and second banquets was deliberate, both on Esther's part and on God's. God wasn't late, nor was He negligent. He was synchronizing the events of His sovereign plan to come together at just the right time for optimal effect. In delaying her request until the second banquet, Esther was being sensitive to God's timing. She was careful not to rush things but to take everything "in His time."

At the table, Esther finally voices her petition. As she speaks, Haman sits in a paralyzed silence, the echo of his wife's words still ringing in his ears (see 6:13b).

> Then Queen Esther replied, "If I have found favor in your sight, O king, and if it please the king, let my life be given me as my petition, and my people as my request; for we have been sold, I and my people, to be destroyed, to be killed and to be annihilated. Now if we had only been sold as slaves, men and women, I would have remained silent, for the trouble would not be commensurate with the annoyance to the king." Then King Ahasuerus asked Queen Esther, "Who is he, and where is he, who would presume to do thus?" Esther said, "A foe and an enemy is this wicked Haman!" Then Haman became terrified before the king and queen. (7:3–6)

A Surprising Climax

When Esther said his name, Haman probably dropped his goblet. In verses 7–10 the drama reaches its climax in a gripping scene of ultimate poetic justice.

> The king arose in his anger from drinking wine and went into the palace garden; but Haman stayed to beg for his life from Queen Esther, for he saw that harm had been determined against him by the king. Now when the king returned from the palace garden into the place where they were drinking wine, Haman was falling on the couch where Esther was. Then the king said, "Will he even assault the queen with me in the house?" As the word went out of the king's mouth, they covered Haman's face. Then Harbonah, one of the eunuchs who were before the king said, "Behold indeed, the gallows standing at Haman's house fifty cubits high, which Haman made for Mordecai who spoke good on behalf of the king!" And the king said, "Hang him on it." So they hanged Haman on the gallows which he had prepared for Mordecai, and the king's anger subsided.

Being Sensitive to God's Interventions Every Day

If you find yourself thrashing about in a lake covered with fog, or maybe just dog-paddling with your head barely above the waterline, here are a few things to remember.

First, *the fog on your lake is not accidental.* Be careful not to make so much noise trying to keep afloat that you can't hear the voice from the shore. While swimming, listen for His voice. It will come in various ways, so you must be intent on hearing it and sensitive to its sound. The voice of God piercing the fog will give you the assurance that your circumstances are not accidental.

Second, *the workings of our God are related to our crises but unrelated to our clocks.* While waiting, look beyond the present. You'll be amazed how it will help you bear the pain.

Third, *the surprises in store are not merely ironic or coincidental; they are sovereignly designed.* While anticipating them, trust Him for justice. Guard against the temptation to question the integrity of the Judge or to impugn His motives.

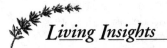
Living Insights

In his excellent book *Waiting: Finding Hope When God Seems Silent*, Ben Patterson concludes with these words. Let's take time to meditate on them.

> The prayer that wrestles with the living God has the faith to believe in the end that even the apparent silence of God is the silence of his higher thoughts and that his no is spoken that he might give us a more resounding yes.
>
> There is a lovely poem which speaks to this wonderfully. It was reputedly written by a young soldier who received massive and permanently debilitating injuries in the Civil War. He lived as a cripple the rest of his days, wrestling and waiting for God to show his face, his purpose in it all. At the end of his strugglings, he wrote this:

> I asked for strength that I might achieve;
>   I was made weak that I might obey.
> I asked for health that I might do greater things;
>   I was given infirmity that I might do better things.
> I asked for riches that I might be happy;
>   I was given poverty that I might be wise.
> I asked for power that I might have the praise of
>   men;
>   I was given weakness that I might feel the
>   need of God.
> I asked for all things that I might enjoy life;
>   I was given life that I might enjoy all things.
> I have received nothing I asked for, all that I
>   hoped for.
> My prayer is answered.

> Such sentiments can be expressed, not at the beginning of our struggle with God, but only at the end. It is a precious intimacy with the heart of God that can see through all of our disappointments the tender and loving hand of God at work for our good. That intimacy comes only after years spent in dialog

with him, a dialog that is sometimes quiet and peaceful and sometimes wrenching and devastating. But through it all there is the same loving God, no matter how we feel him to be at the moment—adversary or advocate, mother or father, friend or enemy. Through it all he is at work for our good, and his victory over us will be also his victory in us when the wrestling is over.[4]

 ## Questions for Group Discussion

1. In our lesson, we read, "Although God is just, He is just in His own time. And in between the ticks of His pocket watch are gaps of silence." Can you pinpoint some gaps of divine silence in your life—times when you yearned for the reassurance of His voice and you heard nothing?

2. How does knowing the difference between our time and God's time help you deal with the enigma of God's silence?

3. Just because God is silent doesn't mean He is absent. And just because there is a delay doesn't mean that God is late. How important was the delay between Esther's first and second banquet?

4. Can you see God working in your "delays"?

5. What does God expect from you while you wait?

6. Previously, Haman occupied the seat of honor, and Mordecai was bound for the gallows. Twenty-four hours later, Haman's lifeless body hung from the gallows, and Mordecai was destined for honor. From this incredible turn of events, what do you learn about how God operates?

4. Ben Patterson, *Waiting: Finding Hope When God Seems Silent* (Downers Grove, Ill.: Inter-Varsity Press, 1989), pp. 147–48.

Chapter 9

AND THE WALLS CAME TUMBLING DOWN

Esther 8

Some walls seem set in concrete and impossible to budge. But if history teaches us anything, it teaches that no matter how intimidating or long-standing, every wall will ultimately fall.

The ruins of ancient walls are strewn amid the rubble of crumbled empires. Egypt. Greece. Rome. All were once imposing world powers whose cities were protected by formidable walls. Now they are simply scenic spots brought to life by travel brochures and tour guides.

No wall loomed as dramatically in our minds as the Berlin wall. For twenty-eight years it divided East and West Berlin, communism and capitalism. It stretched across the city like an ugly gash, its barbed wire forming cruel stitches. Its great masses of concrete seemed immovable. But on November 9, 1989, the wall was pulled down. It collapsed without one shot being fired.

Jericho's wall was similarly imposing. But through a nation that was willing to trust God for impossible things, that wall also came tumbling down (Josh. 6:20).

Other walls, though less tangible, sometimes appear equally impossible to budge. The wall of a critical spirit. The wall of a stubborn will. The wall of an offended friend.

The eighth chapter of Esther is going to teach us some valuable lessons about walls and how to overcome them—even those that appear impenetrable. Whether you're facing a Berlin wall or a wall around someone's heart, remember—there is no wall so strong that God is not stronger still.

Walls That Fell in Esther's Day

There is no scene so dark that God cannot brighten it. There is no law so permanent that He cannot change it. And there is no heart so hard that He cannot soften it. Even if that heart resides in the most powerful person on earth.

An Unchangeable Heart

King Ahasuerus had a vast empire (Esther 1:1–2). His word

was law, which gave him absolute power over his people. This same influential man had promoted Haman (3:1), who then devised a plan to exterminate "a certain people scattered and dispersed" in the empire—a plan the king ratified (3:8–9a, 11). And yet, in Esther 8:1–4, we witness an absolutely amazing thing.

> On that day King Ahasuerus gave the house of Haman, the enemy of the Jews, to Queen Esther; and Mordecai came before the king, for Esther had disclosed what he was to her. The king took off his signet ring which he had taken away from Haman, and gave it to Mordecai. And Esther set Mordecai over the house of Haman.
>
> Then Esther spoke again to the king, fell at his feet, wept and implored him to avert the evil scheme of Haman the Agagite and his plot which he had devised against the Jews. The king extended the golden scepter to Esther. So Esther arose and stood before the king.

The Jews would have been in Haman's hands, but the king gave Haman's estate into the hands of two Jews!

No heart is so hard that God cannot break through it. And if He wants to tear down a "wall," it doesn't matter whether that person is your boss, your mate, your neighbor, or the king of the Medo-Persian Empire.

An Irrevocable Edict

Although the king's heart has softened and Haman has been put to death, Esther must confront yet another wall—the royal edict that is still in effect.

> Then she said, "If it pleases the king and if I have found favor before him and the matter seems proper to the king and I am pleasing in his sight, let it be written to revoke the letters devised by Haman, the son of Hammedatha the Agagite, which he wrote to destroy the Jews who are in all the king's provinces. For how can I endure to see the calamity which will befall my people, and how can I endure to see the destruction of my kindred?" So King Ahasuerus said to Queen Esther and to Mordecai the

Jew, "Behold, I have given the house of Haman to Esther, and him they have hanged on the gallows because he had stretched out his hands against the Jews. Now you write to the Jews as you see fit, in the king's name, and seal it with the king's signet ring; for a decree which is written in the name of the king and sealed with the king's signet ring may not be revoked." (vv. 5–8)

The king's response was extraordinary, especially in light of the law of the Medo-Persians that made royal edicts irrevocable (compare Dan. 6:8, 12, 15). And yet that wall crumbled in the face of another edict.

> So the king's scribes were called at that time in the third month (that is, the month Sivan), on the twenty-third day; and it was written according to all that Mordecai commanded to the Jews, the satraps, the governors, and the princes of the provinces which extended from India to Ethiopia, 127 provinces, to every province according to its script, and to every people according to their language as well as to the Jews according to their script and their language. He wrote in the name of King Ahasuerus, and sealed it with the king's signet ring, and sent letters by couriers on horses, riding on steeds sired by the royal stud. In them the king granted the Jews who were in each and every city the right to assemble and to defend their lives, to destroy, to kill and to annihilate the entire army of any people or province which might attack them, including children and women, and to plunder their spoil, on one day in all the provinces of King Ahasuerus, the thirteenth day of the twelfth month (that is, the month Adar). A copy of the edict to be issued as law in each and every province was published to all the peoples, so that the Jews would be ready for this day to avenge themselves on their enemies. The couriers, hastened and impelled by the king's command, went out, riding on the royal steeds; and the decree was given out at the citadel in Susa. (Esther 8:9–14)

Since the edict of Haman could not be revoked, the king allowed Esther and Mordecai to draft a separate edict. Their edict would not actually annul the first one, but it would annul it in essence by giving the Jews the right not only to defend themselves but to take severe retaliatory action. This countermeasure, along with the death of Haman, would put fear in the enemies of the Jews and avert genocide.

An Impenetrable Gloom

Although Haman was dead, to the Jews his shadow still loomed menacingly across the land. Their days were numbered. They were marked people, targets for destruction. And they were living in a death-row atmosphere of impenetrable gloom.

That is, until they received that second edict.

> Then Mordecai went out from the presence of the king in royal robes of blue and white, with a large crown of gold and a garment of fine linen and purple; and the city of Susa shouted and rejoiced. For the Jews there was light and gladness and joy and honor. In each and every province and in each and every city, wherever the king's commandment and his decree arrived, there was gladness and joy for the Jews, a feast and a holiday. And many among the peoples of the land became Jews, for the dread of the Jews had fallen on them. (vv. 15–17)

Walls that Fall on Any Day

Can you identify with the Jews living under the edict of extermination? Have you felt the cold, hard wall that some powerful person has erected around you, isolating and intimidating you? The bricks of that wall may have been letters or lawsuits or libelous statements in the newspaper. They may have been slurs against your reputation or slander against your character. They may have left you crumbled in a helpless heap, bruised and broken, with your bleeding fists pounding against that wall.

If so, Esther 8 should come as an edict of encouragement. Murderous indictments can be neutralized. What seems permanent can be amended, even nullified, by the countermeasures of God.

Living Insights

Walls take many different forms. Some can be physical, others financial, emotional, spiritual, relational, racial, religious, or marital. What wall do you find yourself up against?

_____

_____

Do you see any way around that wall? What strategies have you tried already? What's been the result?

_____

_____

_____

_____

How frequently do you pray for God to tear down that wall?

_____

_____

How fervently?

_____

_____

It didn't make the headlines, but the story behind the toppling of the Berlin wall is a story of prayer. For ten years Christians gathered in a church in Leipzig, East Germany, to pray for the wall to come down. In the final months before the breakdown of the Communist state and the wall's collapse, thousands of Christians met daily to pray for that end, in meetings that spilled over into gigantic demonstrations.[1]

1. B. Clayton Bell, Sr., "Revolution by Candlelight," *Christianity Today*, April 23, 1990, p. 16.

Tennyson was right.

> More things are wrought by prayer
> Than this world dreams of.[2]

Prayer was not only the force behind the wrecking ball that tore down the Berlin wall, it is also the force that can bring down the walls in your life too. If you need some encouragement in this area, read Luke 18:1–8.

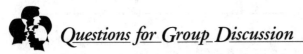

Questions for Group Discussion

1. In the seventeenth century Richard Lovelace wrote: "Stone walls do not a prison make, Nor iron bars a cage."[3] What did Lovelace mean? What kind of wall can imprison a person more than a stone wall?

2. The wall that loomed over the Jews was built on the bedrock of hate and cemented with the mortar of prejudice. Are there any walls that *you* have set up in your life or others'? What materials are they made of?

3. To tear down the wall in Esther's life, God had to first tear down the person (Haman) who had built it. Scary thought. Has God tried to break through the wall of your hardened heart? How did you respond? Has there been a time you surrendered— and were later glad you did?

4. Sometimes we're the ones walled in rather than the wall builders. What principles from Esther's story can help keep your hope alive when you feel like people will never change and the walls will stay forever?

5. It's important to remember that God worked *through* Esther and Mordecai to accomplish His sovereign plan. What part can you play in tearing down the walls in your life (see Matt. 5:23–24; Eph. 4:26–32; Heb. 3:7–8a, 12–13)?

2. Alfred, Lord Tennyson, "The Passing of Arthur," *Idylls of the King,* quoted in *Idylls of the King (and) Camelot* (New York, N.Y.: Dell Publishing, 1967), p. 155.

3. Richard Lovelace, as quoted in *Bartlett's Familiar Quotations,* 15th ed., rev. and enl., ed. Emily Morison Beck (Boston, Mass.: Little, Brown and Co., 1980), p. 296.

Chapter 10

THE LIMITATIONS OF RETALIATION

Esther 9:1–16

Have you ever lost your temper and gone off on a tirade? Have you ever binged while on a diet? Have you ever lost control of your thoughts, when lust or materialism or envy broke out of its harness and ran unbridled through your mind? Have you ever talked too much and later regretted it?

Sure you have. We all have. We've known the pain and regret that come when we let the boundaries of our lives get trampled underfoot.

In this chapter, we want to look at something else all of us have trouble keeping on a short leash—retaliation. We'll discover the solution to this problem in Esther 9:1–16. But before we look at this specific solution, let's briefly examine the problem in general.

The Temptation to Go Too Far

From too many helpings on the all-you-can-eat buffet to exceeding the credit limit on our charge cards, at some time or another we've all gone too far.

We not only go too far in the realms of food and finances, we go too far in the moral realm as well. The saintly apostle Paul himself confessed:

> I don't accomplish the good I set out to do, and the evil I don't really want to do I find I am always doing. (Rom. 7:19 PHILLIPS)

The problem Paul highlighted resides within us all—the universal problem of losing control.

The Key to Holding Back

The answer to our dilemma is as easy to identify as the problem itself. Applying it, however, is a lifetime project. What is the answer? Self-control. One authority described it as follows:

> Self-control is managing our attitudes, feelings,

and actions so they serve our long-term best interests and those of others. Self-control comes to people who learn discipline and social skills. It increases in those who accept God's grace in their lives and who seek to know and apply divine truth in a disciplined manner.[1]

No matter how discouraged you may be about the lack of this quality in your life, there's encouraging news: Self-control is one of the fruits of the Spirit (Gal. 5:22–23). It can be cultivated—even on the most barren branch.

In Galatians 5:23 the Greek term for *self-control* is a combination of two words that we would translate as *strength* and *in*, meaning "inner strength." It describes those who have mastery over their inner desires, whether those desires are sensual or emotional.

Self-control is the key that unlocks the leg irons of slavery to those drives and desires that initially seem to be so freeing and fulfilling. Self-control is to a person what brakes are to a car. Without it, a crash is inevitable.

One of the most difficult times to apply the brakes is when we have the urge to *retaliate*. *Webster* defines the word: "to repay (as an injury) in kind . . . to return like for like . . . to get revenge."[2]

Retaliation is a warlike response between enemies. But notice how General Douglas MacArthur put the brakes on that response once the war between the United States and Japan was over. After World War II, MacArthur modeled great self-control in helping the Japanese rebuild both their country and their dignity. He could have taken his heel and ground it in Japanese soil in revenge for Pearl Harbor. But he chose instead to rebuild.

Joseph showed similar restraint when he had been mistreated and abandoned by his brothers. The cistern and prison he was thrown into could have become seething caldrons of bitterness and resentment. And when he ascended to Pharaoh's court as the second most powerful man in Egypt, he could have deployed a thousand chariots to trample his brothers in the dust. But he didn't. He showed great self-control and blessed them instead.[3]

1. Richard P. Walters, *Counseling for Problems of Self-Control*, Resources for Christian Counseling series, gen. ed. Gary R. Collins (Waco, Tex.: Word Books, 1987), vol. 11, p. 17.

2. *Merriam-Webster's Collegiate Dictionary*, 10th ed., see "retaliate."

3. For some examples of people who exhibited great self-control, read about David in 1 Samuel 24 and 26:1–20, and about Jesus in Matthew 26:62–63 and 27:12–14.

This same quality of self-control is illustrated beautifully in Esther 9:1–16.

The Jews Who Were Freed in Persia

Up to this point in the drama, we have seen God change the heart of a king, which resulted in a change of personnel in the palace. Now we see God pulling the strings to intervene in the fate of the Jewish population living in the Medo-Persian Empire.

Through the edict that Mordecai penned and stamped with the king's signet ring, God gave the Jews the legal right to defend themselves. He allowed them to retaliate and plunder anyone who would attack them (8:11, 13).

Yet in defending themselves, the Jews demonstrated remarkable restraint regarding their enemies' families and possessions.

> Now in the twelfth month (that is, the month Adar), on the thirteenth day when the king's command and edict were about to be executed, on the day when the enemies of the Jews hoped to gain the mastery over them, it was turned to the contrary so that the Jews themselves gained the mastery over those who hated them. The Jews assembled in their cities throughout all the provinces of King Ahasuerus to lay hands on those who sought their harm; and no one could stand before them, for the dread of them had fallen on all the peoples. Even all the princes of the provinces, the satraps, the governors and those who were doing the king's business assisted the Jews, because the dread of Mordecai had fallen on them. Indeed, Mordecai was great in the king's house, and his fame spread throughout all the provinces; for the man Mordecai became greater and greater. Thus the Jews struck all their enemies with the sword, killing and destroying; and they did what they pleased to those who hated them. At the citadel in Susa the Jews killed and destroyed five hundred men, and Parshandatha, Dalphon, Aspatha, Poratha, Adalia, Aridatha, Parmashta, Arisai, Aridai, and Vaizatha, the ten sons of Haman the son of Hammedatha, the Jews' enemy; *but they did not lay their hands on the plunder.*

On that day the number of those who were killed at the Citadel in Susa was reported to the king. The king said to Queen Esther, "The Jews have killed and destroyed five hundred men and the ten sons of Haman at the citadel in Susa. What then have they done in the rest of the king's provinces! Now what is your petition? It shall be granted you. And what is your further request? It shall also be done." Then said Esther, "If it pleases the king, let tomorrow also be granted to the Jews who are in Susa to do according to the edict of today; and let Haman's ten sons be hanged on the gallows."[4] So the king commanded that it should be done so; and an edict was issued in Susa, and Haman's ten sons were hanged. The Jews who were in Susa assembled also on the fourteenth day of the month Adar and killed three hundred men in Susa, *but they did not lay their hands on the plunder.*

Now the rest of the Jews who were in the king's provinces assembled, to defend their lives and rid themselves of their enemies, and kill 75,000 of those who hated them; *but they did not lay their hands on the plunder.* (9:1–16, emphasis added)

The Jews were given legal sanction to utterly destroy their enemies, down to the women and children. They were even given the right to pillage and plunder their material possessions. But notice the Jews' restraint. Nowhere in these verses are women and children mentioned as part of the retaliation—only the men. Also, three times we are told that "they did not lay their hands on the plunder" (vv. 10, 15, 16).[5]

The temptation to go too far must have been great, but the

---

4. Esther was referring here to displaying the bodies of Haman's sons, who had been killed earlier that day.

5. The Jews are careful not to make the same mistake King Saul made concerning the Amalekites, when he disobeyed God and kept the best of the plunder (1 Sam. 15:1–11). Raymond Dillard and Edwin Yamauchi identify the Jews' restraint in Esther "as the antithesis of 1 Sa 15: The narrator is emphatic that the Jews did not take plunder, in spite of the king's permission to do so (8:11). Seizing the plunder 500 years earlier in the battle against Amalek had cost Saul his kingship (1 Sa 15:17–19); here, not taking the plunder brings royal power to Mordecai (vv. 20–23)." Note on Esther 9:5–10, in *The NIV Study Bible,* ed. Kenneth Barker and others (Grand Rapids, Mich.: Zondervan Bible Publishers, 1985), p. 728.

Jews resisted. They pulled in the reins rather than let revenge run through the streets, wild and unrestrained.

Human nature tends to do just the opposite. If the offender strikes, the offended strikes back. But if that cycle is ever to be broken, self-control must intervene and gain mastery over vengeance.

The Christian Who Is Free Today

When you're tempted to take matters into your own hands, to strike back, to get even, there are a few things you should remember.

First, *remember that, as a Christian, you are to be different from the world.*

> Do not be conformed to this world, but be transformed by the renewing of your mind, so that you may prove what the will of God is, that which is good and acceptable and perfect. (Rom. 12:2)

Don't be conformed. Don't let the world squeeze you into its mold. The world's way is to get back. Christ's way is to get us back together (see Matt. 5:38–48).

Second, *remember that, as a Christian, you are a member of a family.*

> For through the grace given to me I say to everyone among you not to think more highly of himself than he ought to think; but to think so as to have sound judgment, as God has allotted to each a measure of faith. For just as we have many members in one body and all the members do not have the same function, so we, who are many, are one body in Christ, and individually members one of another. (Rom. 12:3–5)

As a member of a body, your role is not to take charge but to take directions. It is the head's role to give orders, and the head is the Lord Jesus (see also 1 Cor. 12:12–27, Eph. 4:11–16).

Third, *remember that, as a Christian, the Lord is your defender.*

> Never pay back evil for evil to anyone. Respect what is right in the sight of all men. If possible, so far as it depends on you, be at peace with all men. Never take your own revenge, beloved, but leave room for the wrath of God, for it is written, "Vengeance is Mine, I will repay," says the Lord. "But if your enemy

is hungry, feed him, and if he is thirsty, give him a drink; for in so doing you will heap burning coals upon his head." Do not be overcome by evil, but overcome evil with good. (Rom. 12:17–21)

Restrain yourself when it comes to revenge. The high road of life is not the road of retaliation, it is the road of forgiveness—the road that Jesus traveled when He went to the cross.

Christ also suffered for you, leaving you an example for you to follow in His steps, who committed no sin, nor was any deceit found in His mouth; and while being reviled, He did not revile in return; while suffering, He uttered no threats, but kept entrusting Himself to Him who judges righteously. (1 Pet. 2:21b–23)

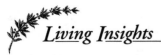

Living Insights

Jesus consistently denounced retaliation. To see how thoroughly He lived the message He proclaimed, read Matthew 26:47–68 and 27:11–54. Jot down several instances in these passages where Jesus could have retaliated but didn't.

1. _____

_____

2. _____

_____

3. _____

_____

4. _____

_____

5. _____

_____

6. _____

_____

Give three reasons why Jesus didn't retaliate.

Isaiah 53:7 _____

_____

1 Peter 2:21 _____

_____

1 Peter 2:23b _____

_____

What positive things happened because Jesus didn't retaliate on the cross?

Luke 23:39–43 _____

_____

Luke 23:46–47 _____

_____

What can we learn from Jesus' example on the cross that will help us in our relationships with others (compare Luke 23:33–37 with 1 Pet. 3:8–9)?

_____

_____

_____

Is there someone who has hurt you? Do you find yourself reliving that scene of hurt in your mind and then retaliating, either verbally or physically? Instead of filling your hands with stones, won't you fold them in prayer (see Matt. 5:43–44)?

 *Questions for Group Discussion*

1. What rights of self-defense did the king's second edict give the Jews (see Esther 8:11)? In light of what the Jews could have done to their enemies, how did they show restraint?

2. Just because we have the right to retaliate doesn't always mean retaliating is the right thing to do. What principles on taking revenge are found in Proverbs 24:29; Romans 12:17–21; and 1 Thessalonians 5:15?

3. In what situations might it be wiser to show restraint, even though retaliation may be justified?

4. Is it possible to get justice without getting even, to vindicate yourself without avenging your enemy? If so, how?

5. In the end, the Jews "had rest from their enemies" (Esther 9:16 kjv)—which was their goal. They fought for the purpose of peace, not punishment. How can the goal of peace help you keep your perspective when confronting an "enemy"?

Chapter 11

AFTER THE ACHE...
CELEBRATE!

Esther 9:17–32

Too often we look at life as a drudgery to be endured rather than a dance to be enjoyed. It seems as if it's easier for us to enter into the eulogies at a wake than the excitement at a wedding, to suffer the aches and pains of life than to celebrate the fun and games. Speaker and author Luci Swindoll writes:

> The highest and most desirable state of the soul is to praise God in celebration for being alive. Without perks our lives are easily lost in the world of money, machines, anxieties, or inertia. Our poor, splendid souls! How they fight for food! They have forgotten how to celebrate. They have forgotten how to request little perks. Our hurried, stressful, busy lives are unquestionably the most dangerous enemy of celebrating life itself. Somehow, we must learn how to achieve momentary slowdowns, and request from God a heightened awareness of the conception that life is a happy thing, a festival to be enjoyed rather than a drudgery to be endured. Life is *full* of perks if we train our souls to perceive them, ". . . a thousand tiny things from which one can weave a bright necklace of little pleasures for one's life."[1]

So true, isn't it? But have you ever thought about why we tend to be uncomfortable with life's little pleasures? Why we seem more comfortable with lamentation than with celebration? Maybe the reason is because we focus on the past with a sigh.

Looking Over the Past with a Sigh

When we walk down memory lane, our thoughts tend to travel down four well-trodden paths. Sometimes those paths turn in a

1. Luci Swindoll, *You Bring the Confetti* (Waco, Tex.: Word Books, 1986), p. 13. Luci is Chuck Swindoll's sister.

melancholy direction, covering the terrain of sad experiences with people, events, circumstances, and decisions.

People

Unfortunately, the people we remember most are often the ones who've hurt us rather than the ones who've helped us, the insensitive rather than the inspirational. For the Jews living in Persia at the time of Esther, Haman was probably the person they would have remembered most.

Events

When we look back at events, our minds tend to catalog catastrophes rather than celebrations. We remember with clarity the Titanic, Vietnam, Watergate, the Challenger disaster. But weddings and births and so many Christmases tend to blur around the edges. We remember the date of the last earthquake, tornado, or hurricane but forget the dates of our children's spiritual birthdays. The same was most likely true in Esther's day. The Jews would have tended to look back to the insidious edict and diabolical plot to exterminate them—and forgotten the details of their deliverance.

Circumstances

Our reminiscences also tend to cluster around certain circumstances. Often those circumstances are wringing wet with blood, sweat, and tears. From divorce to the Great Depression, the memories we hang out to dry are dripping with hardship. The clotheslines in Esther's day were probably no different. The Jews would have remembered the hardship of living on borrowed time . . . slated for destruction, doomed to die.

Decisions

All of us have made wrong decisions in our lives. And many of us are still making monthly payments on those decisions. The bills that come due arrive in the form of shame, guilt, remorse. The accounting was perhaps no different in Esther's day. Think of the decisions King Ahasuerus had made: wanting to display Vashti, possibly in a very humiliating way; waging a disastrous war against Greece; giving the OK to Haman to kill his own wife's people! He must have sighed with regret and disappointment.

The whole point of this meandering trip back in time is this: *Anyone who focuses on the negatives in the past, and keeps focusing on them, will tend to ache rather than celebrate.*

The Book of Esther wasn't written to memorialize the Jews' heartache or their narrowly escaped holocaust. The story of Esther explains how one of the major celebrations in the Jewish calendar, the Feast of Purim, got started. With that in mind, turn your attention to Esther 9, a classic illustration of "ache" turned "celebrate."

Acknowledging the Present with a Celebration

Before we dig into chapter 9, however, let's leaf back a few pages to chapter 3, where we'll discover the origin of this celebration's name.

> Therefore Haman sought to destroy all the Jews, the people of Mordecai, who were throughout the whole kingdom of Ahasuerus.
>
> In the first month, which is the month Nisan, in the twelfth year of King Ahasuerus, Pur, that is the lot, was cast before Haman from day to day and from month to month, until the twelfth month, that is the month Adar. (vv. 6b–7)

The word *Pur* is an ancient word for "lot," similar in concept to our dice.[2] Haman cast these lots to determine what day would be most auspicious for the Jews' destruction.

The date that came up was the thirteenth day of the twelfth month; that is, the month of Adar. But the gears of the universe are not driven by lottery. They're driven by love. And God's love for the Jewish people ground Haman's plans to a halt. In chapter 9, we find that this day of doom was turned to a day of triumph for the Jews. And when the dust had settled and their destiny was safeguarded, a celebration was called for.

> This was done on the thirteenth day of the month Adar, and on the fourteenth day they rested and made it a day of feasting and rejoicing.
>
> But the Jews who were in Susa assembled on the thirteenth and the fourteenth of the same month, and they rested on the fifteenth day and made it a

---

2. The plural form of the word is *purim* (compare Esther 9:24 with 26). In English, we make our nouns plural by adding *s* or *es*. In Hebrew, they pluralize their nouns by adding *im*. For instance, two words depicting angels are *cherub* and *seraph*. Their plurals are *cherubim* and *seraphim*.

day of feasting and rejoicing. Therefore the Jews of
the rural areas, who live in the rural towns, make
the fourteenth day of the month Adar a holiday for
rejoicing and feasting and sending portions of food
to one another. (9:17–19)

What appeared to be a time of extermination turned into a
time of celebration. And it was even named after the very thing
that had first appeared as its death knell: Purim. This feast was a
festive occasion. It was much like the American day of Thanksgiv-
ing when the Pilgrims feasted, giving thanks to God for bringing
them safely to the shores of New England and through the rigors
of a harsh winter.

This groundswell of celebration came from the Jewish people,
but it was Mordecai who made it official.

Then Mordecai recorded these events, and he
sent letters to all the Jews who were in all the provinces of King Ahasuerus, both near and far, obliging
them to celebrate the fourteenth day of the month
Adar, and the fifteenth day of the same month, annually, because on those days the Jews rid themselves
of their enemies, and it was a month which was
turned for them from sorrow into gladness and from
mourning into a holiday; that they should make
them days of feasting and rejoicing and sending portions of food to one another and gifts to the poor.

Thus the Jews undertook what they had started
to do, and what Mordecai had written to them. For
Haman the son of Hammedatha, the Agagite, the
adversary of all the Jews, had schemed against the
Jews to destroy them and had cast Pur, that is the
lot, to disturb them and destroy them. But when it
came to the king's attention, he commanded by letter that his wicked scheme which he had devised
against the Jews, should return on his own head and
that he and his sons should be hanged on the gallows. Therefore they called these days Purim after
the name of Pur. And because of the instructions in
this letter, both what they had seen in this regard
and what had happened to them, the Jews estab-
lished and made a custom for themselves and for

their descendants and for all those who allied themselves with them, so that they would not fail to celebrate these two days according to their regulation and according to their appointed time annually. So these days were to be remembered and celebrated throughout every generation, every family, every province and every city; and these days of Purim were not to fail from among the Jews, or their memory fade from their descendants. (vv. 20–28)

Just as Jews treasure the ceremonies that bring their past to life, so many Americans treasure Washington, D.C., with its national monuments. Our capital is replete with testimonies to the past, like the Washington Monument and the Lincoln Memorial. The masoned stones and chiseled marble give us places where we can read, remember, and reflect on the noble and heroic. They give the past perspective and significance. And they turn our sighs into smiles of gratitude.

Facing the Future with a Reminder

The establishment of Purim as a perennial custom took place in verses 29–32.

> Then Queen Esther, daughter of Abihail, with Mordecai the Jew, wrote with full authority to confirm this second letter about Purim. He sent letters to all the Jews, to the 127 provinces of the kingdom of Ahasuerus, namely, words of peace and truth, to establish these days of Purim at their appointed times, just as Mordecai the Jew and Queen Esther had established for them, and just as they had established for themselves and for their descendants with instructions for their times of fasting and their lamentations. The command of Esther established these customs for Purim, and it was written in the book.

To this day, Purim is celebrated every year among the Jewish people. An air of fun and festivity fills the synagogues as children come dressed as their favorite character from the story. When the Book of Esther is read, everyone participates by rattling noisemakers, booing, and stomping their feet every time Haman's name is mentioned and cheering at the names of Esther and Mordecai.

Throughout the day, messengers, who are often in disguise, deliver trays of food and delicious confections to neighbors and those in need.

Instead of looking back with a heavy sigh or a saddened heart, the Jews treat Purim as a time of fun and feasting and giving gifts.

What does all this say to us today? When most of us think back on the past, our thoughts are tinged with remorse and disappointment. Thumbing through the photo albums of our minds, the details of the past may fade around the edges, while the mistakes we made stand out in sharp relief. But those photos should not discourage us. As we look at ourselves today, we should be encouraged that we're different people than we were back then. We've changed. We've grown. We've learned from our mistakes—hopefully.

Just remember: Unending remorse and shame never made anyone better or brought anyone to maturity.

If the past makes you squirm, let us give you two pieces of advice. One is a suggestion. The other is a warning.

The suggestion is this: *Raise up a mental memorial to turn your sadness into celebration.* A story about a small town in Alabama illustrates the point. One year, the farmers of the area were anticipating a bumper crop of cotton. But then the boll weevil invaded the fields and destroyed the economy in that small rural town. Not to be defeated, one of the farmers got the idea of planting peanuts instead, a crop that the boll weevil won't touch. The idea caught on and, before long, the economy recovered. The town later came to be known as Enterprise, Alabama. And do you know what they did? They raised a monument to the boll weevil! It's there to this day. Isn't that great?

On the heels of that suggestion comes a warning: *Don't turn your memorial into a shrine.* The memorial is merely a reminder. It isn't an end in itself, but a means of turning our thoughts toward the good that the mental monument represents.

An example of a monument turned to a shrine is found in 2 Kings 18:4. The bronze serpent that God used to bring healing to any Israelite who had been snakebitten (see Num. 21:4–9) had been preserved as a memorial; but it later became revered as a shrine, and the Israelites even burned incense to it.

So remember, after the ache—celebrate! But don't let the celebration become an end in itself. Like the celebration of the Lord's Supper, it should be a memorial—not a shrine.

Living Insights

Do you look back on the past with a sigh in your heart or with a song?

All of us have skeletons in our closets that rattle in shame over our past. But those memories are not there to haunt us. They are there to help us—help us learn, understand, forgive, love, do what's right, make restitution if necessary, and trust God for strength and for healing.

When God looks at our lives, He looks at them through the clean lenses of forgiveness. Take David, for example. He was a great king, but he fell into adultery and committed murder (2 Sam. 11). Yet the New Testament calls him a man after God's heart (Acts 13:22) and places him in the Hall of Faith in Hebrews 11 (vv. 32–34). Why? Look at Psalm 51 and you'll see.

David looked back on his past with shame and remorse. Indeed, it *was* a shameful and remorseful past. But he didn't spend the rest of his life cowering inside, crippled by guilt. He did something positive about it. He confessed the sins of his past and accepted God's forgiveness (compare 2 Sam. 12:13 with Ps. 51).

If things from your past come back to point an incriminating finger at you, won't you take them to the Lord and deal with them once and for all? Here are some passages that should encourage you: Psalm 103:8–14; Isaiah 1:18; 1 John 1:9.

Now take one negative memory that has been haunting you and turn it into something positive. Out of the rubble of regret, build a monument to God's grace in your life. Describe the negative memory to God and ask Him to use it for good in your life (see Rom. 8:28).

If He has already done this, write down how He transformed the bad into good—this can be your written monument. Then take a few minutes to pray, scaling every step of that memorial with praise for what God has done—and is doing—in your life.

Questions for Group Discussion

1. When you think back on your life, do you tend to focus on the successes or the mistakes? The joys or the hurts?

2. We can't change the past, but we can change our view of the past. How do you think God sees your past? What does He focus on?

3. What if you viewed your life through God's eyes? How would that new perspective on the past change your present?

4. The story of Esther was recorded so that when future generations of Jews recalled their people's exile, they would focus on the relief, not the hardship. And they would praise God for His faithfulness. Do you have a story of God's faithfulness that you might like to pass on to future generations of your family?

5. Family stories of determination, courage, and answered prayer are like the mental memorials that give us a sense of history and identity, inspiring faith and providing a set of unchanging values. What are some other advantages of keeping the stories alive in your family?

6. Through festivals, the Jews have been keeping their stories alive for thousands of years. What if your family declared its own Purim-type holiday to remember God's faithfulness? What story would be the centerpiece of your celebration? How could you make the day meaningful . . . and a lot of fun?

Chapter 12

In the End, God Wins

Esther 10

One of the reasons it is possible to go on in spite of struggles and disappointments and heartaches is because we know that in the end, God wins.

Before we get to that triumphant ending, however, we have to plod through some difficult chapters in our own lives. Chapters where the plot is convoluted. Where pleasure comes only in short sentences. And where pain often forms rambling paragraphs that go on, page after page.

Though the syntax of suffering may grate against our earthly ears, and though the vocabulary of heaven may sometimes be beyond our understanding, the story of life does come together in the end. As God's children, we will indeed live happily ever after.

No matter what tragedies we have had to endure, God will triumph over those tragedies in the end.

The Book of Esther stands on history's shelf like a condensed version of life itself. Though the fate of God's people hung precariously in the balance, in the end God triumphed over the impending tragedy.

A Few Scenes of the End, ahead of Time

To some, all this talk about God winning in the end sounds like fairy-tale thinking. But it is not a pie-in-the-sky, by-and-by type of hope. It is a hope grounded in the truth of Scripture.

> "And He will wipe away every tear from their eyes; and there will no longer be any death; there will no longer be any mourning, or crying, or pain; the first things have passed away." (Rev. 21:4; see also John 14:1–3; Rom. 8:18; 2 Cor. 4:16–18; 2 Tim. 4:7–8)

Heaven will be a paradise illumined by the glory of God, where joy will echo through the corridors of the Father's house. Sin, in all its twisted and grotesque forms, will be forever barred from our eternal estate.

Due to the absence of sin, there will be holiness. Without pain and suffering, there will be perfection. With the final defeat of

Satan, there will be relief and peace. With our new natures and glorified bodies, there will be unity and harmony. With the glory of God radiating resplendently throughout heaven, there will no longer be a need for lesser luminaries like the sun and moon. And with death defeated, immortality will reign. God will be "all in all" (see 1 Cor. 15:22–28).

This sovereign assurance of a happy ending prepares us for the closing chapter in the ancient story of Esther.

A Final Glimpse at the Story, after the Fact

The final chapter in Esther functions like an epilogue, enshrining the hero in an encapsulated tribute.

> Now King Ahasuerus laid a tribute on the land and on the coastlands of the sea. And all the accomplishments of his authority and strength, and the full account of the greatness of Mordecai, to which the king advanced him, are they not written in the Book of the Chronicles of the Kings of Media and Persia? For Mordecai the Jew was second only to King Ahasuerus, and great among the Jews and in favor with his many kinsmen, one who sought the good of his people and one who spoke for the welfare of his whole nation. (Esther 10:1–3)

The story ends with the same king, the same kingdom, the same country, the same realm of authority, and the same manner of ruling. But unlike the beginning of the story, there has been a major change around the throne. Mordecai has replaced Haman. The presence of evil and corruption and wicked plans is out. Wholeness, peace, and greatness are in.

The last verse informs us that Mordecai has been promoted to second in command and explains why. First, he was "great among the Jews." Second, he was "in favor with the multitude of his kinsmen." Third, he "sought the good of his people." And fourth, he "spoke for the welfare of his whole nation."

Mordecai's promotion was a testimony to God's sovereign care of His people. Mordecai was a Jew in a Gentile country, a country where the Jews had originally come as captives. A comparison of verses 1 and 3 reveals the stark contrast. Verse 1 simply mentions King Ahasuerus, without reference to his race. Verse 3 reads,

"Mordecai the Jew." A Jew being in such a high political position within a Gentile kingdom could only have happened because God was in charge.

From this small chapter, three potent principles emerge.

Principle one: *When God wins, He often uses unexpected people.* Who would have guessed that the one-time servant at the king's gate would be described the way he is in 10:2? Mordecai's promotion from such humble beginnings is reminiscent of David's ascent from shepherd to king (see Ps. 78:70–72).

In using the most unlikely of people to bring about His victory, God brings into sharp relief the greatness of His sovereign power. For example, He took Moses, an eighty-year-old Jew with a criminal record—not a thirty-year-old West Point wiz—and through him pulled off the Exodus.

The list of unlikely recruits goes on and on. Who would have used a harlot to hide Jewish spies (see Josh. 2:1–20)? Who would have used a rebel prophet to spearhead an evangelistic crusade in Nineveh (see Jon. 1–4)? Who would have used a Pharisee and a persecutor of Christians to pen most of the New Testament and plant churches (see Acts 26:1–20)? Or who would have used a deserter as the major spokesman of the early church (see Acts 2:14–42; Gal. 2:7–8)?

Principle two: *When God wins, the qualities He upholds are usually unpretentious.* When the curtain falls on the last scene in the story of Esther, it comes down on a man who stands center stage in the drama but who bears the marks of true humility. Look at how he is described: "in favor with his many kinsmen" and "one who sought the good of his people" (Esther 10:3).

What a beautiful, flesh-and-blood incarnation of the truth found in Philippians 2:3–4.

> Do nothing from selfishness or empty conceit, but with humility of mind regard one another as more important than yourselves; do not merely look out for your own personal interests, but also for the in-terests of others.

Nothing is more Christlike than occupying one's space in lowli-ness of mind and true servanthood (see Matt. 20:28; Luke 22:24–27; John 13:1–17; Phil. 2:5–8).

Principle three: *When God wins, the message He honors most often is universal.* God honors those who have vision, who look beyond

91

themselves to look out for others. Mordecai worked, as we have already noted, for the good of "his people"—he "spoke for the welfare[1] of his whole nation" (Esther 10:3b).

Mordecai's world was vast, not limited by the sidewalks and street corners of his own neighborhood. His concern was for the Jews in the entire empire, all 127 provinces, not just his family and friends in the citadel of Susa.

Also, by virtue of seeking the *shalom* of his people, he would necessarily have to seek the good of the Persians with whom the Jews lived. Perhaps in the back of his mind were Jeremiah's words to the first exiles under Babylon's domination:

> "Seek the welfare of the city where I have sent you
> into exile, and pray to the Lord on its behalf; for in
> its welfare you will have welfare." (Jer. 29:7)

Thinking beyond our own national or spiritual group reflects God's heart for the world. His desire is for people of every tribe, every tongue, and every nation to know His peace (see Phil. 2:9–11; 1 Tim. 2:4).

Unfortunately, like Haman, our present-day world doesn't honor these principles; it doesn't think like this at all. Which creates a struggle between those who would follow God's principles and those who would oppose them.

A Futile Struggle with God's Plan, Now and Then

Why does our world struggle against God's principles? Three reasons stand out.

When the world selects its major players, the criteria are much different. The chosen ones look good; they have the right degrees and impressive credentials. They sound right and fit the mold of the successful. Because this selection process is so pervasive, it's important to remember: God's choices are often unexpected (1 Sam. 16:7).

When the world looks for qualities that will get a big job done, the externals get the nod. Those who are dressed for success, those with personality and pizzazz are usually the ones given the next rung up

---

1. The Hebrew word for "welfare" here is *shalom*. It is "one of the most theologically significant words in the OT, occurring 237 times. It can mean 'absence of strife, war'; but 'completeness,' 'wholeness,' 'harmony,' 'fulfillment' more accurately encompass the meaning of the word." F. B. Huey Jr., "Esther," in *The Expositor's Bible Commentary*, gen. ed. Frank E. Gaebelein (Grand Rapids, Mich.: Zondervan Publishing House, 1988), vol. 4, p. 839.

on the corporate ladder. But before you take that next step, remember: God upholds the unpretentious and humble (James 4:6).

When the world arranges its priorities, first and foremost it looks out for number one. The heart of the world is the self—self-protection, self-promotion, and self-absorption. But don't let the egocentric universe exert any gravitational pull on you. Remember: God's concern is universal. His message reaches out to the whole world (Luke 2:29–32; John 3:16; 1 John 2:2).

Fulfilling Hope for the Christian, in God's Time

All of this is reminiscent of something that happened in a small hamlet outside Jerusalem, in Bethlehem. It was there that God chose to enter the human race. And the vehicle through which He chose to arrive? A young Jewish girl who got pregnant out of wedlock and became the scandal of Nazareth.

You'd have thought God would have come to Jerusalem through the loins of royalty. But He didn't. He came unexpectedly—in His time and in His way.

And you'd have thought that the birth would have taken place in the imperial palace or at some sprawling estate, crawling with servants. But it didn't. There was not even room in a common inn. The Son of God was born in a barn and cradled in a feeding trough that was cushioned with straw.

And to whom did that little one come? Simply to Mary and Joseph? To His Nazarene neighborhood? No. "God so loved *the world,* that He gave His only begotten Son . . ." (John 3:16a, emphasis added). And those who believe "have eternal life" (v. 16b).

So in the end, not only does God win, but we do too!

As we reach the end of the Book of Esther, let's join commentator John A. Martin as he reflects on some of the lessons Esther teaches about the goodness of God's providential care.

> As the original Jewish readers read this account they would have been struck by the way God was sovereignly protecting them, often when they did not even know it. Many things in the Book of Esther happened that were beyond anyone's control except that of God, who oversees history. And the Book of Esther is filled with irony, with ways in which events turned out unexpectedly and in favor of God's people. Queen Vashti, a Persian, was deposed so that Esther,

a Jewess, could become queen and save her people. Haman, once exalted, was brought low, and Mordecai and the Jews, once hated, were exalted and honored. A decree that would have wiped out the Jews was overruled by one which led to the destruction of nearly 76,000 enemies of the Jews. No wonder Purim was celebrated yearly with such rejoicing: to help the Jews remember that God is in control and that people should faithfully worship and serve their great God.[2]

Living Insights

The Book of Esther is a poignant study of the silent government of God, referred to theologically as *providence*. The *New Dictionary of Theology* gives us a good working definition of this doctrine.

> Providence is the beneficent outworking of God's sovereignty whereby all events are directed and disposed to bring about those purposes of glory and good for which the universe was made.[3]

God directs *all* events? Yes—as the apostle Paul writes, God "works all things after the counsel of His will" (Eph. 1:11b). Let's search the Scripture to find out what we can about the extent of God's providence.

Scripture	Extent of God's Providence
Psalm 104:24–30	
Matthew 10:29	

2. John A. Martin, "Esther," in *The Bible Knowledge Commentary*, Old Testament edition, ed. John F. Walvoord and Roy B. Zuck (Wheaton, Ill.: Scripture Press Publications, Victor Books, 1985), p. 713.

3. *New Dictionary of Theology*, ed. Sinclair B. Ferguson, David F. Wright, and J. I. Packer (Downers Grove, Ill.: InterVarsity Press, 1988), see "Providence."

Scripture	*Extent of God's Providence*
Matthew 10:30	_____
	_____
Job 12:23	_____
	_____
Psalm 139:16	_____
	_____
Galatians 1:15–16	_____
	_____
Psalm 121	_____
	_____

Now look up Romans 8:28–30 to see what is taught about God's providence in the life of the believer. How can *all* things work together for good in our lives, even the bad things?

_____

_____

_____

What is the ultimate good—the light at the end of the tunnel—toward which our lives are moving?

_____

_____

In his book *Where Is God When It Hurts*, Philip Yancey gives us some illuminating words for times when life's tunnel seems too dark, too narrow, and too long for us to carry on.

> [God] has allied Himself with the poor and suffering, establishing a kingdom tilted in their favor, which the rich and powerful often shun.
> He has promised supernatural strength to nourish our spirit, even if our physical suffering goes unrelieved.

He has joined us. He has hurt and bled and cried and suffered. He has dignified for all time those who suffer by sharing their pain.

He is with us now, ministering to us through His Spirit and through members of His body who are commissioned to bear us up and relieve our suffering for the sake of the head.

He is waiting, gathering the armies of good. One day He will unleash them. The world will see one last explosion of pain before the full victory is ushered in. Then, He will create for us a new, incredible world. And pain shall be no more.[4]

Fairy tales aren't the only stories that end "happily ever after." Because of God's providential care, Esther's story ended that way . . . and so will ours someday.

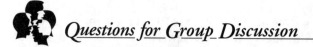 *Questions for Group Discussion*

1. As we stand back and view the complete tapestry of Esther's story, several themes emerge in the shades and patterns. Though His name is never mentioned, what attributes and characteristics of God does the story reveal?

2. Can you see a shadow of Christ in the story, specifically in Esther's actions?

3. How did the events of Esther keep alive the flame of the Messianic hope within the Jewish heart?

4. How do the events of Esther keep alive the hope of Christ's Second Coming within your heart?

5. In the book of Esther, no heavenly hand scrawled, "Haman is a liar!" on the throne room wall. No mysterious voice emanated from a burning bush to tell Esther what to do. And no Red Sea parted for the Jews to pass through before crashing over their enemies. Even so, Esther witnessed God's hand at work—through open doors, uncanny coincidences, and amazing turns of events.

---

4. Philip Yancey, *Where Is God When It Hurts* (Grand Rapids, Mich.: Zondervan Publishing House, 1977), pp. 182–83.

Can you see God's hand at work in your life in similar ways?

6. Based on Esther and Mordecai's example, what kind of person is God looking for in our generation—"for such a time as *this*" (Esther 4:14, emphasis added)?

7. What can you do today to become that type of person?

BOOKS FOR
PROBING FURTHER

The Book of Esther is like a prism. Hold it up to the light and you can see a rainbow of brightly colored subjects. The spectrum ranges from the courage of the queen to the silence of heaven; from the cruelty of hatred to the faithful providence of God.

Should you want to study any of these subjects in greater detail, we have provided a list of books for your further reading.

Courage

Andrew, Brother, with Dave and Neta Jackson. *A Time for Heroes.* Ann Arbor, Mich.: Servant Publications, Vine Books, 1988. The Book of Esther drips with the heroism of Esther and Mordecai— ordinary people who changed the course of history. Today we live in an age depleted of heroes, yet Brother Andrew asserts that every Christian is called to greatness. He takes us on a tour of the Scriptures, pointing out heroes from the past along the way. By highlighting these men and women, the author shows how God crafts heroes from the same ordinary mud and mortar of which *we* are made.

Johnston, Jon. *Courage.* Wheaton, Ill.: Scripture Press Publications, Victor Books, 1990. When Esther stood up for her people, she risked her life. Her courage, however, averted a holocaust and forever enshrined her as a Jewish heroine. In this well-written book, the author calls believers to face their fears and demonstrate the courage of their convictions—just as Esther did.

The Silence of Heaven

Carlson, Dwight, and Susan Carlson Wood. *When Life Isn't Fair.* Eugene, Oreg.: Harvest House Publishers, 1989. Like Mordecai and Esther, this father and daughter faced a deadly enemy together. The foe was leukemia, which Susan contracted in her early twenties. Here we relive their experience—their fears, their searching questions, and ultimately their conclusions about who God is and the assurances you can cling to when life isn't fair.

Jacobs, Joy. *When God Seems Far Away*. Wheaton, Ill.: Tyndale House Publishers, 1988. Joy Jacobs has experienced distance from God—distance often caused by her own fear, guilt, inadequacy, anger, and doubt. She has also bridged that distance and learned to embrace God. Through a reflective study of the Hebrew names for God, she shows how we, too, can bridge that distance.

Marshall, Catherine. *Light in My Darkest Night*. Old Tappan, N.J.: Fleming H. Revell Co., Chosen Books, 1989. A series of devastating events that culminated in the death of her baby granddaughter threw Catherine Marshall's faith into a tailspin. She cried out to God in her agony and in her anger, yet for all her tears, she received only the hollow echo of her own prayers bouncing off heaven's gate. In this honest and intimate book, the author offers hope to anyone who has ever experienced spiritual silence.

Patterson, Ben. *Waiting*. Downers Grove, Ill.: InterVarsity Press, 1989. Subtitled *Finding Hope When God Seems Silent*, this book deals with the emotions experienced when we feel God has placed our lives on hold. The author explores the mystery of waiting and the wisdom of God in making us wait. Exploring the lives of two men who had to wait, Job and Abraham, Patterson unearths two golden treasures required for successful waiting—humility and hope.

The Providence of God

Berkouwer, G. C. *The Providence of God*. Translated by Lewis B. Smedes. Grand Rapids, Mich.: William B. Eerdmans Publishing Co., 1952. This theological text is the second volume in the series *Studies in Dogmatics*. With careful scholarship and sparkling clarity, this theologian conducts a thorough study of how God rules and watches over His creation. The author examines biblical texts, church history, and contemporary scholars to construct a compelling case for God's providence, which pervades the Book of Esther.

Sproul, R. C. *The Invisible Hand: Do All Things Really Work for Good?* Dallas, Tex.: Word Publishing, 1996. A highly respected theologian, R. C. Sproul brings the often overlooked doctrine of providence to the common person as rich and reassuring truth. By revealing God's behind-the-scenes direction in the lives of Bible heroes as well as his own life, he demonstrates that God is truly *for* us. Our lives aren't products of blind chance. We can learn to rest in the invisible hand of God.

Commentary on Esther

Huey, F. B., Jr. "Esther." *The Expositor's Bible Commentary.* Gen. ed. Frank E. Gaebelein. Grand Rapids, Mich.: Zondervan Publishing House, 1988. Volume 4. The author provides a thorough study of the Book of Esther with helpful background material and in-depth analysis of key Hebrew words.

The Jewish Purim Festival

Want to find out more about how the Jews celebrate Purim? From the ancient rituals to the boisterous traditions to the delicious foods, all can be found by exploring the following web site: www.holidays.net/purim.

Some of the books listed may be out of print and available only through a library. For those currently available, please contact your local Christian bookstore. Books by Charles R. Swindoll may be obtained through Insight for Living. IFL also offers some books by other authors.

To purchase more copies of this study guide or to request an IFL catalog and further information about our ministry, please call:

United States
1-800-772-8888

Canada
1-800-663-7639

Australia
(03) 9877-4277

ORDERING INFORMATION

ESTHER: A WOMAN OF STRENGTH AND DIGNITY
Cassette Tapes and Study Guide

This Bible study guide was designed to be used independently or in conjunction with the broadcast of Chuck Swindoll's taped messages which are listed below. If you would like to order cassette tapes or further copies of this study guide, please see the information given below and the order form provided at the end of this guide.

		U.S.	Canada
EST	Study guide	$ 4.95	$ 6.50
ESTCS	Cassette series, includes all individual tapes, album cover, and one complimentary study guide	30.95	44.50
EST 1–6	Individual cassettes, includes messages A and B	6.00	7.48

Prices are subject to change without notice.

EST   1-A: *God's Invisible Providence*—Survey of Esther
      B: *There She Goes . . . Miss Persia!*—Esther 1:1–2:7

EST   2-A: *Strength and Dignity on Parade*—Esther 2:8–20
      B: *An Evil Interlude*—Esther 2:21–3:15

EST   3-A: *Thinking and Saying What's Right—Regardless*—Esther 4
      B: *Esther's Finest Hour*—Esther 5

EST   4-A: *What Goes Around, Comes Around*—Esther 6
      B: *God's Surprising Sovereignty*—Esther 7

EST   5-A: *And the Walls Came Tumbling Down*—Esther 8
      B: *The Limitations of Retaliation*—Esther 9:1–16

EST   6-A: *After the Ache . . . Celebrate!*—Esther 9:17–32
      B: *In the End, God Wins*—Esther 10

HOW TO ORDER BY PHONE OR FAX
(Credit card orders only)

Web site: http://www.insight.org

United States: 1-800-772-8888 or FAX (714) 575-5684, 24 hours a day, 7 days a week

Canada: 1-800-663-7639 or FAX (604) 532-7173, 24 hours a day, 7 days a week

Australia and the South Pacific: (03) 9877-4277 from 8:00 A.M. to 5:00 P.M., Monday through Friday.
FAX (03) 9877-4077 anytime, day or night

Other International Locations: call the International Ordering Services Department in the United States at (714) 575-5000 from 8:00 A.M. to 4:30 P.M., Pacific time, Monday through Friday
FAX (714) 575-5683 anytime, day or night

HOW TO ORDER BY MAIL

United States
- Mail to: Mail Center
    Insight for Living
    Post Office Box 69000
    Anaheim, CA 92817-0900
- Sales tax: California residents add 7.75%. Texas residents add 8.25%.
- Shipping and handling charges must be added to each order. See chart on order form for amount.
- Payment: personal checks, money orders, credit cards (Visa, MasterCard, Discover Card, and American Express). No invoices or COD orders available.
- $10 fee for *any* returned check.

Canada
- Mail to: Insight for Living Ministries
    Post Office Box 2510
    Vancouver, BC V6B 3W7
- Sales tax: please add 7% GST. British Columbia residents also add 7% sales tax (on tapes or cassette series).
- Shipping and handling charges must be added to each order. See chart on order form for amount.
- Payment: personal cheques, money orders, credit cards (Visa, Master-Card). No invoices or COD orders available.
- Delivery: approximately four weeks.

Australia and the South Pacific
- Mail to: Insight for Living, Inc.
  GPO Box 2823 EE
  Melbourne, Victoria 3001, Australia
- Shipping: add 25% to the total order.
- Delivery: approximately four to six weeks.
- Payment: personal checks payable in Australian funds, international money orders, or credit cards (Visa, MasterCard, and Bankcard).

United Kingdom and Europe
- Mail to: Insight for Living
  c/o Trans World Radio
  Post Office Box 1020
  Bristol BS99 1XS
  England, United Kingdom
- Shipping: add 25% to the total order.
- Delivery: approximately four to six weeks.
- Payment: cheques payable in sterling pounds or credit cards (Visa, MasterCard, and American Express).

Other International Locations
- Mail to: International Processing Services Department
  Insight for Living
  Post Office Box 69000
  Anaheim, CA 92817-0900
- Shipping and delivery time: please see chart that follows.
- Payment: personal checks payable in U.S. funds, international money orders, or credit cards (Visa, MasterCard, and American Express).

Type of Shipping	Postage Cost	Delivery
Surface	10% of total order*	6 to 10 weeks
Airmail	25% of total order*	under 6 weeks

Use U.S. price as a base.

Our Guarantee: Your complete satisfaction is our top priority here at Insight for Living. If you're not completely satisfied with anything you order, please return it for full credit, a refund, or a replacement, as you prefer.

Insight for Living Catalogs: The Insight for Living catalogs feature study guides, tapes, and books by a variety of Christian authors. To obtain a free copy, call us at the numbers listed above.